Transition to the
Golden Age in

2032

Diana Cooper

Transition to the Golden Age in

2032

DIANA COOPER

FINDHORN PRESS

ISBN 978-1-84409-558-2

Edited by Sabine Weeke and Carol Shaw
Proofread by Cynthia Barralis
Cover, interior design and illustrations by Damian Keenan
Printed and bound in the European Union

1 2 3 4 5 6 7 8 9 10 11 12 14 13 12 11

Published by
Findhorn Press
117-121 High Street,
Forres IV36 1AB,
Scotland, UK

t +44 (0)1309 690582
f +44 (0)131 777 2711
e info@findhornpress.com
www.findhornpress.com

Transition to the Golden Age in

2032

DIANA COOPER

FINDHORN PRESS

Contents

Foreword 13

SECTION 1 – The Transition

1   General World Forecasts 2012 – 2032 19
2   Spiritual Influences in 2012 23
3   Spiritual Influences from 2012 to 2032 26

SECTION 2 – Updated Forecasts for Individual Countries

4   Europe – An Overview 30
5   Forecasts for Countries of Europe 32

    Andorra 32
    Austria 33
    Bosnia 34
    Croatia 34
    Cyprus 35
    Czech Republic 35
    Estonia 36
    France 36
    Germany 37
    Greece 38
    Holland – The Netherlands 39
    Hungary 39
    Ireland 40
    Italy and the Vatican 40
    Latvia 41
    Poland 41
    Portugal 42
    Romania 42
    Slovenia 43
    Spain 43
    Switzerland 43

Contents

	Turkey	44
	United Kingdom	45
	Scandinavia	
	Denmark	48
	Finland	48
	Norway	48
	Sweden	49
6	The Middle East – An Overview	50
7	Forecasts for Countries of the Middle East	52
	Bahrain, Kuwait, Oman, United Arab Emirates, Libya, Qatar	52
	Bahrain	53
	Dubai	53
	Iran	54
	Iraq	54
	Israel	55
	Libya	55
	Saudi Arabia	56
8	Asia – An Overview	57
9	Forecasts for Countries of Asia	58
	Afghanistan	58
	India	59
	Pakistan	60
	Tibet	61
10	Forecasts for Countries of the Far East	62
	China	62
	Japan	65
11	Africa – An Overview	69
12	Forecasts for Countries of Africa	71
	Egypt	71

Contents

	Mali	72
	South Africa	73
13	South America – An Overview	74
14	Forecasts for Countries of South America	76
	Brazil	76
	Chile	76
	Guatemala	77
	Honduras	77
	Mexico	77
	Peru	77
15	Russia and Mongolia	79
	Russia	79
16	Australasia and The Pacific Islands	82
	Australia	82
	New Zealand	83
	Fiji	84
	Honolulu	85
	The Pacific Islands	85
17	Arctic, Antarctic, Canada	86
	The Arctic	86
	The Antarctic	87
	Canada	87
18	USA – An Overview	89
19	Forecasts for the States of America	94
	Alabama	94
	Alaska	94
	Arizona	95
	Arkansas	95

Contents

California 96

Colorado 96

Connecticut 97

Delaware 97

Florida 97

Georgia 98

Hawaii 98

Idaho 99

Illinois 99

Indiana 99

Iowa 99

Kansas 100

Kentucky 100

Louisiana 101

Maine 101

Maryland 102

Massachusetts 102

Michigan 102

Minnesota 103

Mississippi 103

Missouri 103

Montana 104

Nebraska 104

Nevada 104

New Hampshire 105

New Jersey 105

New Mexico 105

New York 105

North Carolina 106

North Dakota 107

Ohio 107

Oklahoma 107

Contents

Oregon 108
Pennsylvania 108
Rhode Island 109
South Carolina 109
South Dakota 109
Tennessee 110
Texas 110
Utah 110
Vermont 111
Virginia 111
Washington 111
West Virginia 112
Wisconsin 112
Wyoming 112

20 The Caribbean 113
Barbados and St. Kitts 113
Cuba 113
Jamaica 113
Trinidad 114

SECTION 3 – Preparation for The Transition

How to Prepare Yourself for
The Transition into The Golden Age 116
Epilogue 129

Appendix
The 12 Spiritual Chakras of the Planet 133
   Map 134
The 33 Cosmic Portals 136
   Map 138

Foreword

Nearly thirty years ago I was at rock bottom in my life and could see no future for myself. Despite having no religious or spiritual background I called out for help – and an angel appeared to me and took me on a journey to show me my future. This encounter set me on a spiritual path, which has not always been easy but which I have remained determined to follow.

Ten years after their first visit, the angels returned to ask me to tell people about them. At their direction I wrote my first book, *A Little Light on Angels* (the new edition is called *A New Light on Angels*), and since that time these luminous beings have appeared in most of my writings.

A few years later, my guide Kumeka connected with me and I have worked with him ever since. Kumeka originates from another universe but came to this one to help with the setting up of the fifth experiment of Atlantis, which resulted in the Golden Age. Since then, he has returned here at significant times in the history of the planet to assist us. I now know that Kumeka is my twin flame. We come from the same planet and have the same Monad or I AM Presence. He has never been incarnated but when I have incarnated he has guided me. He has had to 'find' me in each lifetime; in other words, he could not guide me until my light has become bright enough for him to see me.

Because he has never had a physical body he is a hard taskmaster, having no idea what physicality and emotions are. He does not realize that I need a rest after flying half way round the world and giving lectures every day on a tour!!! However, he is always there when I need him and he does provide awesome information. Furthermore, I totally trust him.

If he thinks I am not listening to him carefully enough, or he really wants to gain my attention, he tweaks my physical body. For a horrible six months he gave me excruciating sciatica whenever he wanted to speak to me. As he often did this while I was driving, I dreaded going any distance because I would suddenly be hit by sharp pain and have to stop the car to shake out my leg. It took me some time to realize that it was Kumeka doing this and I was not very pleased with him when I found out! We had a discussion during which he agreed that he would refrain from giving me sciatica but instead would buzz my left ear if he wanted my attention. Other Masters and Angels talk into my left ear too. For my part, I agreed to listen carefully. I have not had a single twinge of sciatica since.

The other mighty illumined being who gives me information and is constantly with me is the Universal Angel Metatron. He does not come from this universe either but is in charge of the ascension of this planet into the new Golden Age. He is helping individuals to open their Stellar Gateway chakras and is working with the planetary Stellar Gateway chakra. Metatron's energy is bright golden orange and he and his angels often impress themselves into photographs as Orbs to help us with our ascension paths. Metatron draws attention to his presence by buzzing my right ear. He is the only being who uses this ear, and when he does so it is often quite a sharp pain. This is when he is using angel sonics to break up any resistance I may have to his message.

Everyone in the whole world has guides and angels helping them on their path, and when we recognize these beings our lives become filled with joy. I feel very blessed to have such wonderful guides and angels with me.

I am not great at meditation. Sitting cross-legged in front of a candle is fine for a short while but aching knees and back significantly reduce my chance of entering the silence. Instead, I find that I receive downloads while walking in my local conifer forest. Also Kumeka, Metatron or one of the other angels or Masters pop in with comments or information at unexpected times. I try to remain alert to their promptings as much as possible.

One of the most encouraging things to happen in the next twenty years is the opening up of the religions to higher spirituality. All dogma is based on fear and this will change into love. The awakening of the portal in

Mesopotamia will return self-worth to the Arabs and help to dissolve the dogma of Islam, enabling its followers to embrace their religious beliefs in a spiritual way. Christians will no longer talk about the fear of God but will enjoy the love of God. Jews will learn humility and will seek peaceful solutions. Many Masters, such as Catherine of Sienna, Mary Magdalene and Saint Theresa of Avila are stepping forward to help all religions become spiritual for the New Golden Age.

In 2009, when I wrote *2012 and Beyond*, I was filled with enormous excitement at the great spiritual opportunities ahead. There are amazing and extraordinary energies coming in at this time to propel us through the twenty-year transition period into the new Golden Age. After that book came out so many people contacted me, wanting to know what the forecast was for their country that I tuned into the forecasts for the whole world again.

As I discuss in this book, some of the forecasts, such as the major floods in Australia, have already happened because the cleansing has been brought forward. And a forecast is simply that – an intimation of the probability based on the current consciousness. We can change it all by raising our consciousness further and further.

The Transition

CHAPTER 1

General World Forecasts
2012 – 2032

A forecast is the likely outcome based on the situation and mindset of the people at a given time. A forecast, therefore, is not set in stone. People are changing and moving rapidly in their ideas and consciousness, and this affects future outcomes.

Lightworkers have been focussing healing, light, love and joy into many dark places, and in doing so dissolving the karma and shifting the negative energy. This means that cleansing is no longer needed in these places, and a much more positive outcome becomes possible.

One example for this is Poland: the heavy energy and continued energizing of the horrific past in Auschwitz have been holding the country back for years. Many groups of people have gone into the area and put in much light, which has purified the space for a time. Then others arrive with doom, gloom and judgement and fill it with darkness again. However, the area is getting lighter now because so many people have sent in pure energy, and the more we can do this, the less cleansing will be needed in the future.

In addition to this, the oversouls of several countries have been calling cleansing forward. Pakistan was full of warlike egos and ancient karma, which needed much purification. It was originally forecast that this would take place around 2017. However, the oversoul of the country recognized the importance of the changes ahead and wanted to embrace fully the double dimensional shift on Earth. So it asked for the cleansing to start ahead of time to allow people to wake up. The horrific floods in 2010 are the first stages of this change.

19

There are many influences on the world that we are not aware of. The influx of millions of angels, the re-incarnation of many evolved souls and the opening of ancient portals and sacred sites full of wisdom will have a massive effect on the planet. Also, many energies were placed into the ground in ancient times, which will awaken during the transition to assist humanity in making the necessary shift.

~ *World Economy* ~

The world has never before experienced a shift like the current one that will turn us inside out. Economies will change dramatically during the transition, until money no longer has relevance. Dinosaur businesses out of tune with the new paradigm will collapse and be replaced by smaller ventures working for the good of the animals, people and the planet. By 2020, the governments everywhere will curb the power of the banks and many big corporations will be struggling for their viability. They will fight back stealthily and secretly by trying to create global governments, but eventually the rising consciousness will sweep them away.

People power will have an increasing influence on decisions, which have always been the province of banks, big business and governments.

From a higher spiritual perspective, the recession and financial problems of the world are false, created by the decisions of governments worldwide. World debt is not actually a debt but a deficit as the money owed is illusory. We are trying to solve something that cannot be solved, so we need to be ready to adjust worldwide. China holds 'false wealth' based on illusory money. Like banks, they are not playing with real money but with promises. They are killing the environment to produce this illusion, which cannot be fed back to the people in a tangible form. World debt would be quite simple to resolve by not trying to pay back. Corporations would not like it because they do not want to lose power. This overall economic situation needs a global agreement, and for this the countries of the world need to trust each other.

As money has less viability, creativity, music, art and sport will be honoured again. People will start to take responsibility for their own health and healing using natural methods. A big brother state will no longer be acceptable to our societies. Sharing, caring and community will take us into the fifth dimension.

~ Unemployment and what to do about it ~

For generations people have been doing unpalatable jobs solely to earn money and keep a roof over their heads. Because this is no longer in tune with the new energy sweeping the planet, the Higher Selves of many are calling on them to find work that makes them feel alive and full of joy; that harnesses their creativity and enables them to live in the fifth dimension. As a result, such souls are finding themselves made redundant or otherwise without work. Many spend hours running round in circles applying for jobs similar to the ones they have left; this, though, is wasted energy. They are being called upon to do spiritual work on themselves to raise their frequency. When their vibration matches that of their perfect soul work, the right employment will automatically find them.

Archangel Gabriel, in charge of the cosmic portal of Mount Shasta in California, brings clarity. If this is your dilemma, one thing you can do is to ask each night before you go to bed to visit Gabriel's retreat during your sleep to receive purification and clarity about your divine right path. You can also meditate daily with Archangel Gabriel for this.

Another way of calling forward the right work for you is to remember what brought you great joy when you were a child. Before you were squashed into an adult world, what was your vision? What did you really want to do? Even if you cannot see how it can earn you a living, start doing more of it. If you are almost aligned to your soul purpose, this will have an effect very quickly. If you are not, you may need some patience. But the universe will inevitably carry you forward in the right direction.

~ Health ~

Throughout the world there will be more stress, caused by the economic falseness, causing people to turn to alcohol, drugs etc. Others will create self-sustaining communities, where friendship and happiness will offset the stress.

Health will be different everywhere in the world, for in some places, such as Africa and India, there will be famine unless we change our energy and open our hearts.

If we all stop focussing on a false situation and instead focus on alternative solutions, better education and shared consciousness, we can transform the possibilities for humanity and for the planet. For this, we need to develop trust between and within nations. This may get worse before it gets better, but by 2020 people everywhere will be working together.

~ Tools to help ~

1. Learn to be self-sufficient. Grow vegetables, learn about hens and plant trees.
2. Walk more and use bicycles.
3. Build up a bank of kindness within your community by noticing and honouring good deeds, so that people have a sense of goodwill and want to help each other.
4. Bless all water.
5. Get to know your neighbours.
6. Eat local produce.
7. Connect with elementals and angels.
8. Look at and connect with the stars.
9. Be grateful every day.
10. Meditate.
11. Love each other.
12. Love yourself.

CHAPTER 2

Spiritual Influences in 2012

The transition refers to the twenty-year period between the old third- to fourth-dimensional age on Earth ending in 2012 and the new fifth-dimensional one starting in 2032.

2012 marks the end of a 260,000-year cosmic era on Earth. It is an incredibly important time, because new energies are entering the planet and huge vibrational shifts will take place in that year. Nearly seven billion souls have been given permission to incarnate now, so that they have the opportunity to experience the challenges available to accelerate their spiritual growth. A vast number of them will return to spirit before 2032 to share their experiences with their home planets.

These are the spiritual influences that will affect the world in 2012:

1.   The twelve fifth-dimensional planetary chakras are opening and connecting to the wisdom of their stars.

They will powerfully affect the areas they are located in as well as the world as a whole. The more people who awaken spiritually and work with their own personal fifth-dimensional chakras, the easier the transition will be for the whole planet. These are the locations of the planetary chakras:

1.   The Earth Star chakra is in London, United Kingdom.
2.   The Base chakra is in the Gobi Desert, China.
3.   The Sacral chakra is in Honolulu, Hawaii.

4. The Navel chakra is in Fiji.
5. The Solar Plexus chakra covers the whole of South Africa.
6. The Heart chakra is in Glastonbury, United Kingdom.
7. The Throat chakra is in Luxor, Egypt.
8. The Third Eye chakra is in Afghanistan.
9. The Crown chakra is in Machu Picchu, Peru.
10. The Causal chakra is in Tibet.
11. The Soul Star chakra is in Agra, India.
12. The Stellar Gateway chakra is in the Arctic.

2. Thirty-three cosmic portals are opening and flooding their areas in the Christ light.

The Christ light is a golden energy, carrying wisdom, healing, protection and unconditional love, which will spread into the earth and to the people. It dissolves the old and enables people to attain higher frequencies.

3. Many other sacred sites and portals are starting to open.

Many of the sacred sites and portals in the world have been closed or only partially open. Their awakening will accelerate in 2012, and it will influence the people. Examples are the Table Mountain in South Africa and Uluru in Australia. Even the great, two-way interdimensional portal of Stonehenge, United Kingdom, has only been partially open. Most of the sacred sites, pyramids and portals in China have been closed and will have a profound influence when they open, though it may cause some confusion.

4. The wisdom of the seventh-dimensional chakra of Hollow Earth, where the entire knowledge of our world is stored, is becoming available to us.

The centre of the planet holds a seventh-dimensional paradise known as Hollow Earth. It is one of the Golden Cosmic Keys to the universe and contains the Great Pyramid of Hollow Earth, where all the information and wisdom of every civilization, Golden Age, portal or kingdom in the history of Earth is held. As people start to connect with this, the entire universe will come into attunement and harmony.

5.   The wisdom of the crystal skull of Thoth will start to be accessed.

During the Golden Age of Atlantis, the High Priest Thoth programmed a crystal skull with the wisdom and knowledge of his tribe. This will start to become available in 2012 and profoundly affect methods of healing and wholeness on the planet.

6.   There is a cosmic moment at 11.11 a.m. local time on 21st December 2012, when pure Source energy is available to those who are tuned in.

There is a preparatory cosmic moment on 11-11-2011, which will allow Source energy to be accessed for a few instants. However, the 2012 cosmic moment is the one that has been forecast by all the wise ancients, including the Mayans. At this moment, the portals of heaven open and unimaginable light will pour in.

CHAPTER 3

Spiritual Influences from 2012 to 2032

1. **The Great Pyramid in Hollow Earth will start aligning with the Great Pyramids in the centre of each of the stars to bring the universe into alignment by 2032.**

When the spiritual heart centre of the planet in Glastonbury, United Kingdom, awakens in 2012, it will connect to the cosmic heart and ignite the crystal pyramids of Atlantis, which are spread around the universe. This will enable the heart centres of all the planets, stars and galaxies in this universe to connect. This massive wake-up will bring all the stars, planets and galaxies of this universe into alignment by 2032. Then the entire universe will become fifth-dimensional.

2. **Those who were incarnated in Lemuria will wake up and start to activate the Lemurian crystals to heal the planet.**

Aeons ago, Lemurians created extremely powerful healing crystals. They were specifically programmed to help with the twenty-year transition.

3. **2012 marks the start of the ascension of all the universes.**

During the twenty-year transition, each of the twelve universes will move to a faster frequency. The twelfth-dimensional universe will merge with the Godhead. The first-dimensional universe will become second-dimensional, and so on. A new first-dimensional one will be created.

Our planet is currently in a fourth-dimensional universe, which is moving into the fifth dimension by 2032. Earth has been holding our universe back, as it has been vibrating at a third-dimensional frequency until recently. In 2010, we attained the fourth dimension because enough people opened their hearts. During the transition, we must speed up to the fifth dimension. We will have to raise our frequency very rapidly.

Time frame

2012   End of 260,000-year outbreath

2012 – 2023 Eleven-year inbreath. This is like the preparation for a house move, when everything is sorted before it is either packed for the next stage or thrown away. Everything that has been hidden away or lost is brought to the surface and examined. The attics and cellars are cleared out as well as the cupboards in the living quarters. We will see the impact on the planet as the clearout starts, and have an opportunity to use our energy to cleanse the world rather than be cleansed.

2017 – 2022 Main cleansing of the planet. During this period, nature will use the elements to finally purify any area where there are still lower energies.

2023 – 2032 Nine-year pause to prepare for 2032.

~ What happens in 2032? ~

A new fifth-dimensional blueprint is put into place for our planet and our entire universe. Everything — trees, flowers, animals, fish, humans — will speed up in frequency.

My guide Kumeka gave me an invitation to visit Source in my sleep, in order to celebrate my life. I asked to go there, and when I woke in the morning I was held in the palest pink pearl light,

which stayed with me. As I took my morning walk in the woods,
I breathed the pale pink pearl light out to the trees and flowers.
To my delight, one of my little fairy friends came skipping up to
me to ask me to do this whenever I could, as it was helping the
flowers to ascend to a higher frequency.

During this period, those souls who cannot maintain at least a fourth-dimensional energy, with their heart open and some spiritual understanding, will choose to leave. If they originate in this universe, they will return to the inner planes for further education. If they come from another universe, they will return to their home planet there.

In addition, many fourth- and fifth-dimensional souls will decide to 'go home', if they can be of more assistance from there.

There will be a considerable exodus as souls have learnt all they need to from Earth.

Updated Forecasts for Individual Countries

CHAPTER 4

Europe

An Overview

~ Weather ~

Over the years the weather will change and fluctuate, some areas becoming much dryer, others flooding. There has been a great deal of pollution in some parts, and this will be cleansed slowly by the higher energy coming in and by many high-frequency portals here. Where land needs to be cleansed, this will mainly be achieved by flooding and all low-lying areas are at risk. We can also anticipate unexpected earthquakes, high winds and fires, even where they have never been evident before.

~ Economy ~

Economically, the double-dip recession anticipated will cause hardship to the masses. Throughout Europe and elsewhere, people will be so enraged by the greed of the bankers that eventually this anger will boil over. Then governments everywhere will eventually curb the power of the banks. By 2020, people will be appalled by what was allowed to happen.

Also by 2020, individuals will no longer look to insurance companies for security. Self- responsibility will reign, and people will start to form self-help communities.

Here as in other parts of the world, by 2032 food and water will be more important than cash.

~ *Spiritual Influences* ~

Europe is in the charge of Archangel Raphael, the emerald-green angel of healing. This continent is constantly changing, so there are many different energies here. Spiritually, living in Europe shakes people up and opens their chakras, and this is enabling more people to connect with their guides and angels. It is a very interesting continent to live in for spiritual growth.

There are three cosmic portals opening in Europe. These will bring in the Christ light and spread it across the continent.

The first is in York/Yorkshire Dales, United Kingdom, spreading a pure and gentle light.

The second is in Andorra, and this will particularly impact Spain with its high-frequency energy.

The third one is in the sea off the coast of Marseilles. Linking with the retreat of Mary Magdalene, it will powerfully influence the world, affecting the thinking of the masses with waves of divine feminine wisdom.

There are also many other portals and sacred sites fully opening throughout Europe, which will raise the frequency of the people quite significantly and quickly.

CHAPTER 5

Forecasts for Countries of Europe

~ *Andorra* ~

The 26ᵗʰ cosmic portal carrying the Christ energy is found in the mountains of Andorra. It has been sleeping and will be opening in 2012. This portal is under a fire sign and it is guarded by dragons, who are fourth-dimensional elementals. They are here to offer eternal strength and protection to those who have courage in their hearts. Those who are worthy will find that the dragons become their friends and companions, who will guide their evolution and bring them prosperity. They will spread an understanding of abundance in accordance with spiritual law for the highest good of all.

People throughout the world will tune into Andorra to connect to the fire dragons and to work with them. This portal will affect each person differently. Tune into it when you are ready and it will show you who you truly are. It will also introduce you to the wonder of space, the universe and the spirit world.

This higher energy will cleanse and purify the corruption and negativity that has been associated with Andorra. Then the beauty and dragon energy within the mountains will enable the country to shine and be truly abundant. By 2022, it will find its true soul expression.

~ *Austria* ~

The culture and beauty of Vienna brings light to this charming country. The economy has been sensibly handled, so there is not too much financial karma. However, there are some things holding Austria back. This country holds a fear of being manipulated by other nations, especially Germany, and so losing its identity. In addition, there is still guilt held in the collective consciousness about the Austrians' part in World War II. This can only be cleared if enough people do spiritual work to dissolve it.

> *I facilitated a seminar in Austria in 2009. At that time, the forecast was that Austria would not have completed its karma from the war by 2012 and this would hold the country back. However, we did healing on the karma during the seminar, and many of those who took part have continued with the spiritual work. I am told that Austria's karma will now be completely cleared by 2012. This is such a wonderful reminder that we can make a difference. We have the power to change everything and allow the world to go through an easy transition. Every thought you have, every decision you take can make a difference.*

In the mountains of Austria, the energy is pure and clear, and the forests of this country are holding the light. However, there is a pass in the mountains through which people escaped from Austria to Switzerland; the sadness and loss of these people leaving their homeland is still held in the land here, and this needs cleansing.

Sound is held within the mountains of the world. This is especially true of the Alps in Austria, as this country is particularly in tune with sound, and it is this that will bring purification here.

Throughout much of Austria, there is a homely feeling as family is important. Because of this, fifth-dimensional communities will start easily here. There will be a relatively easy transition, and after 2032 Golden Cities will rise up.

~ Bosnia ~

The cruelty and pain of war still hangs like a grey pall over the entire land. Even in the mountains where energy is usually pure and clear there is grief and anger, which needs to be healed. Fear and rage have haunted Bosnia for centuries, allowing the bully/victim-scenario to develop, and this resulted in horrific genocide, which scarred the land. Underlying this savagery, played out differently by each side, is a huge fear of total loss and anger about oppression and mistrust.

The whole world that looked on and ignored the situation bears karma for its lack of action, so collectively much is owed to this part of the world. Now at last, all sides are beginning to take responsibility for themselves and take mastery over their destinies. Much cleansing and healing will be needed by earth, air, fire and water. However, the sheer beauty of the land and the resilience of the citizens are already bringing laughter and hope into this part of the world.

The people of Bosnia will be quite slow in moving into fifth-dimensional communities because they want to experience individuality and independence first.

Each person who invokes the angels of love, peace, abundance and joy and asks them to sing over this country is helping to redress world karma.

~ Croatia ~

The people of Croatia are wary. The fear of loss and subjugation motivates their actions but healing is beginning to take place in the soul of Croatia. As this country is now stepping into true freedom and regaining its confidence, its inner beauty is growing. The long coastline is helping to purify the land. By 2032, it will be a fifth-dimensional place to live in and the people will automatically attract abundance.

~ Cyprus ~

Cyprus has a gentler energy than its neighbour, Greece, and carries less karma.

However, there is stuck energy in the buffer zone between Turkish and Greek Cyprus. This zone has not been inhabited for over thirty years but needs to be cleansed of the spirits of those who died here and others who have gravitated here waiting to pass over. On the other hand, it is wonderful to see the way nature has started to claim the area and create a safe haven for creatures and plants. This is bringing much light to this place.

Cleansing has already started in Cyprus. The mudslide of 2009 was intended as a wake-up call.

The High Priestess Aphrodite is very linked into this island, and her love energy will spread peace and a sense of brotherhood/sisterhood so that this country can flow into the fifth dimension.

~ Czech Republic ~

This country nestles in the heart of Europe and has been subjected to war and oppression for centuries. Lack of confidence and self-worth as well as fear of self-expression in the collective consciousness of the people has enabled this to happen. At last, this is coming to an end.

The Czech people are travelling widely to work and bring back confidence as well as money to enrich their country. Their self-esteem is growing individually and as a nation.

In addition, the opening of the cosmic portal off the coast of Marseilles will affect this country considerably, bringing in the gentler wiser energy of the divine feminine. So will the expansion of the portal of Lourdes, for Mother Mary's healing light will enfold the Czech Republic in love and peace.

The snow-covered mountains have helped to keep the energy here as high as possible in the circumstances. In the future though, melting snow will cause flooding, which will finally cleanse both the ancient and more recent karma in the land.

~ *Estonia* ~

Estonia still has grey energy as it struggles to be free and independent once more. It will be influenced by the opening of the cosmic portal in the North Pole as well as by the gentler energy of the York portal and the bright clear energy of that at Omsk. Together these will influence the people and return their sense of confidence and well-being.

~ *France* ~

Because much of France is rural, the greed and corruption mainly found in cities has been contained. Those people who live a simpler lifestyle will find the transition years easier than those who dwell in cities, especially if they are already self-sufficient. Many will flock to the French Alps where people will awaken and even start to hear angels singing.

A huge spiritual opening is expected for France. Under the water off the coast of Marseilles, a new cosmic portal is opening soon after 2012. This portal will enormously change the consciousness of the masses, who will become receptive to new spiritual understanding. Those living in the countryside will open their hearts to the town dwellers who are displaced in the cleansing, which needs to take place.

Marseilles also holds the retreat of Mary Magdalene, which contains her gentle and light but strong energy. It is bright yellow and enhances good feelings, which will enable relationships to become stronger and more meaningful. When its light touches a person they will be able to let down their guard and be themselves. This will enable many to have deep nourishing partnerships even though they have never done so before. It will also encourage people to speak their truth.

In addition, the vast and wondrous Universal Angel known as Mother Mary has her retreat at Lourdes. Her influence is already felt in France but it will become even stronger, and healing, compassion and love will spread from this area. The influence of these portals will soften the resistance to change and allow the French to embrace the new. This country will start to co-operate with other countries including its traditional foes, while still keeping its uniqueness.

~ *Germany* ~

The last of the darkness of the wars must be cleansed from the land, so unexpected weather conditions will occur, which will cause the old to be transmuted. Germany has a dual role.

It is the Keeper of the Fifth-Dimensional Light for the planet. This includes a golden key to the thirty-three cosmic portals, and as a result Germany is working in alignment with Archangel Sandalphon, who is the doorkeeper to Hollow Earth. This country has earned this role since the Second World War for the way it has handled the merging of East and West Germany in a fifth-dimensional way.

The guilt, which is held in its collective consciousness, will be totally cleared in 2012. Guilt always attracts punishment, and when the old feelings of guilt finally resolve there will be an overwhelming sense of relief and self-worth. Then this country can take its place to spearhead the move to enlightenment and ascension.

Thousands of mature and wise souls have chosen to incarnate here since the Second World War, both to help mitigate old karma and to hold this higher light for the landmass of Europe.

Many scientists and technologists in Germany are working with Master Hilarion, Chohan of the Fifth Ray of Technology and Science to bring forward spiritual technology for the New Golden Age.

Some, whose bodies were used for experiments during the war, have reincarnated again. They still hold fear at a cellular level but this time they are allowing their bodies to be used for cellular light healing, which will clear all karma and bring total health and healing. This will happen consciously and also unconsciously in their sleep time. This time, Germany will lead the world in cellular light healing technology and freely offer it to the world. It will transform people everywhere.

Through this healing work, this country will be offered divine grace. In addition, this focus on healing will bring peace into the collective heart of Germany, so that the land and everyone in it will rise quickly into the fifth dimension. This will make the twenty-year transition period easier here than in many places.

There is much cosmic wisdom held by the trees in the Black Forest, and this will anchor and maintain higher energy in Germany during the changes. Many fifth-dimensional communities will form here, and after 2032 new Golden Cities will arise in this country.

~ *Greece* ~

The Greeks have a huge pride in their ancient heritage. This underlies a disappointment in themselves that somehow they are not fulfilling their potential, which makes them defensive. The karma of their past acquisitions will be repaid by 2012, while their glorious cultural and spiritual heritage remains a source of inspiration to many.

The islands are pure and clear but there will be some cleansing by fire and earthquake on the mainland. However, it will be relatively little, just enough to bring humility and openheartedness to the people.

The most important factor to influence Greece will be the waking-up of the dormant kundalini within the cosmic pyramid constructed here at the fall of Atlantis. This pyramid was originally built by the High Priest Poseidon of Atlantis with the help of the Goddess Athena and contains much ancient wisdom. The entire construction was totally devastated by an earthquake many centuries ago. Nevertheless, the energy remains, as does its connection with the constellation of the Pleiades. The Parthenon has been built on the site.

The tribe led here by the High Priest Poseidon at the fall of Atlantis brought with them great knowledge of medicine and healing, much of which was received through their connection with the Pleiades. As the energy of 2012 wakes up the lost energy within this area, the Greeks will start to remember their ancient inheritance. Eventually, this country will be amongst those who lead the world in natural forms of health and healing.

They will teach people everywhere how to make whole the mental, emotional, spiritual and physical bodies of people and animals through divine resonance. This will be achieved through herbs, music, crystals and other methods. This country will also be influenced by the cosmic portals in Mesopotamia and the Sphinx. It will also be touched by the opening of the thirty-third portal in the North Pole, which carries more Christ light than any other portal.

At last, the grace and wonder brought here by Poseidon's tribe at the fall of Atlantis will be restored, and a great Golden City will arise after 2032.

~ Holland – The Netherlands ~

Over recent years, evolved, liberal, tolerant souls have incarnated here, and there are many enlightened people in the population.

This country has always had an intimate knowledge of water and the oceans. The Dutch East India Company was founded on this. Paradoxically, their development of a fleet and some of its policies earned the Netherlands karma, while water has cleansed the land over the centuries.

In more modern times, their social policies, including the integration of foreigners, have meant karma has been balanced. However, this country lies very low and much of it will disappear under water by 2032. Many of its citizens will move to higher areas of Europe and take their wisdom with them. They will find innovative ways to build homes on the water, and will develop leading technology and construction methods for this, which will be copied worldwide.

~ Hungary ~

The karma of times prior to known history has attracted attack to this flat and landlocked place. Battered by war and defeat, ruled by oppressors, this country has continued to survive and to maintain charming villages and a family tradition. Its grey aura will be healed soon after 2012, and people will feel safe again.

The spillage of toxic sludge in 2010, which so devastated the rivers and polluted the Danube, was a big wake-up call and shock. It is hoped this will propel the Hungarian people to value nature and focus on cleansing their waterways.

Hungary will draw energy from the portal of Marseilles, and that will finally end the old. By 2032, fifth-dimensional communities will form here quite naturally, and peace and contentment will reign.

~ Ireland ~

There is still much anger and fear in Ireland as a result of religious splits in the past and the terrorist activities of recent years. It is a country with many wounds that need to be healed.

Within the collective consciousness of Ireland is a feeling of helplessness about the potato famine of 1845-52, a time of mass starvation. The famine was caused by the English burying their plague victims on the ley lines, thus blocking them, so that the potato crops failed. Unconsciously, the Irish knew this. The English then behaved very badly, and ire against England is still held in the Irish collective psyche. The Irish are now, at last, beginning to forgive and release the whole situation, so that Ireland can reach its true spiritual potential and light in the next few years.

The countryside of Ireland holds much Celtic magic. There are powerful stone circles and sacred sites, many only partially awake waiting to open in 2012 or soon after. There is much religious dogma here and there is also spiritual purity. The whole country is alive with angels, unicorns and elementals. The magical, mystical qualities of the land and the high spiritual light of the Irish will propel the country through the transition years.

Ireland is a country of warm-hearted welcoming people, and this special quality will help them be a beacon of light to the world in the future.

~ Italy and the Vatican ~

Much beauty is held in Italy, for so many Renaissance sculptors and artists chose to work in this country, raising the frequency enormously. In their creations, these people captured and held the energy of the Cherubs, energy fragments of the Cherubim, as well as unicorns and angels. This has helped to hold Italy in the light.

As the energy frequency rises, the huge corruption here will be revealed in the light and the people will demand integrity. Then people of honour will step forward to lead. The power of organizations like the Mafia will disappear, as their vibration will be too low to attract supporters or people to terrorize.

If the Roman Catholic Church remains intransigent and rigid, it will implode and the Vatican will collapse. If it opens up to higher spirituality, it will blossom.

Gradually, true spirituality and the true glory of Christ's message will emerge here.

~ Latvia ~

This country has a grey aura as it tries to shake off the shackles and find its self-worth again. The cosmic portals of the North Pole, York and Omsk will influence the land and its people, helping them to find confidence and courage. Then this area will start to shine.

~ Poland ~

Hitler took Poland first because he knew there would be less resistance. This was because it was not a democracy and the people were used to being given orders. While the Polish people still fought and defended themselves, the Nazis found it easier to conquer them than a nation of individuals who were used to speaking up for themselves.

The darkness of Auschwitz has been affecting Poland. The concentration camp has been kept alive to serve the memory of the horror with the intention that it will never be repeated. However, people have been focussing on the darkness and therefore energizing and continuing it. This has held Poland back. Meanwhile, however, many lightworkers have been focussing light, love and joy into Auschwitz, and soon after 2012 it is expected to be clear. This will help the whole world.

Poland has moved away from communism and oppression but there is still a grey feeling, which needs cleansing. The people are held back by poverty consciousness and a lack of self-worth held in the collective consciousness. At last, they are starting to change this and attract more abundance and joy into their lives, but it has been a slow process. Now, many are moving collectively into self-responsibility and mastery.

The United Kingdom and other countries bear karma towards Poland because they did not protect this country sooner. This has partly been repaid economically by Polish workers migrating and taking home knowledge and confidence – but more is needed.

This country will receive light directly from the thirty-third portal at the North Pole. All the cosmic portals carry the Christ light, but thirty-three is the number of the Christ consciousness and holds the strongest energy. Also, the Source light pouring through the Stellar Gateway in the Arctic will profoundly affect Poland and help it rise to the fifth dimension.

~ *Portugal* ~

The people here as elsewhere in many parts of Europe are disillusioned by the moral corruption of its leaders and businesses. They are starting to ask questions and the rising consciousness will demand change. Despite resistance on the part of the establishment, transformation will take place in every area of life here.

The colonial acquisitions of the 15th and 16th century enriched the country financially and culturally but created much karma, which is yet to be worked out. It should be cleared soon after 2012.

This country will be greatly influenced by the energy coming from Fatima, where Archangel Raphael and his twin flame, the Universal Angel Mother Mary, are very influential. Love, healing, abundance and great light will sweep across the land and Portugal will be transformed by 2032.

~ *Romania* ~

Ancient karma held in this landlocked country has held it back, for it has been constantly invaded and war-battered. This has dented the aura of Romania, so that it has lost its direction, its self-worth and purpose. Fortunately, in the snow-covered mountain ranges the energy is high, and this has helped to maintain the dignity of the people, who are very proud of their ancestral heritage. Old karma will end soon after 2012, and it will be cleansed in a number of ways. Grace in the form of angelic intervention will help to dissolve ancestral karma and heal the hearts of many. In addition, there will be some flooding due to snow melting as well as fire and earth movement. This country lies between the cosmic portal of the

Arctic, the Stellar Gateway of the planet in the Arctic and the portal at the Sphinx, and this light pouring in will awaken the ancient wisdom held in the mountains. Then their frequency will change dramatically and Romania will automatically attract abundance and regain self-esteem.

~ Slovenia ~

The Slovenian people are naturally warm, welcoming and homely. Many have open hearts for love and caring is in the soul of this country. But they hold in their collective consciousness a huge fear of not being good enough. This unworthiness has its origin in ancient karma. Older souls who carry peace in their hearts are now incarnating here. These will influence everyone and eventually lead the country into hope and abundance. Then its outer and inner beauty will shine.

~ Spain ~

Spain is a vast country that will see many changes for it has very mixed energies. As the weather becomes more extreme, people will move into the mountains. Many churches hold gold and other treasures purloined from the Aztecs and Incas. When the energy of this is cleansed, much disbelief and confusion will be experienced. Also the pain of the Spanish Inquisition is still held in the land, which must be purified.

The pilgrimage route known as the Camino Santiago runs across Spain, and the constant procession of pilgrims has created a powerful ley line of great light. This allows wisdom and knowledge from Hollow Earth to be accessed. When the cosmic portal in Andorra opens, it will send light through Spain. Fifth-dimensional communities will form in the mountains.

~ Switzerland ~

There are two things holding Switzerland back. The first is the Large Hadron Collider beneath the Franco-Swiss border near Geneva. It is the world's largest and highest-energy particle accelerator, and already its construction has cracked the Earth's crust.

The second is the karma that has accrued because the Swiss banking system has colluded for years to allow greedy and dishonest people to hide and hold onto their ill-gotten gains. Wealth that has been stolen or accumulated through the disempowerment or slavery of others is dark energy, which will be cleansed by the elements. This must be swept away for the new to arise; thus unexpected earthquakes and flooding will cleanse this negativity, unless the people of Switzerland and the world purify it soon.

This precept also applies to Liechtenstein and other places that are protecting dark financial energies. However, many highly evolved souls are incarnating in Switzerland, with an understanding of spiritual law and the integrity to make the changes needed.

In the mountains, the energy is very pure, so fifth-dimensional communities will be formed here. The sonics of the angels light up the mountains.

~ *Turkey* ~

Ancient guilt from the days of the Ottoman Empire has been held in the soul of Turkey. The last of this karma will be released soon after 2012, and the people, who will start working together in harmony, will feel this as a relief. Women will claim their power and this will help Turkey spiritually, politically and economically.

It is the guilt of the old karma that has caused the people to feel undeserving. Guilt always results in punishment, so this feeling within the energy field of Turkey has resulted in this country being treated with a lack of respect by the world. Once it will have been cleansed, Turkey will again regain its sense of power and worth, which will automatically attract abundance. The light and ancient wisdom held in the mountains will then be released.

In addition, when the portal of Mesopotamia opens, it will greatly affect Turkey and remind its soul of its greatness. This country will emerge as a beautiful and gracious fifth-dimensional country.

~ *United Kingdom* ~

The United Kingdom is not ready for 2012. The Earth Star chakra is located in London but that city is not yet spiritually prepared for it to awaken and open by 2012. The excitement, joy, celebration and love of two billion people focused onto London during the wedding of Prince William and Kate made a massive impact, but this was unfortunately counteracted by two things. One was the core of people angrily resistant to the celebration, and the other the frisson that touched millions of people when the fear of God was mentioned during the service.

It is now hoped by the spiritual hierarchy that a huge burst of light generated by the excitement of the Olympic Games in 2012 will make London ready, so that it can ground the energy for the new age. I have heard people saying ominously that there is trouble brewing for the Olympics but my guidance is that it will go smoothly if we let it. So it is up to us what happens. How to help London, the Earth Star Chakra of the Planet, for 2012:

1. Light candles and send love and light to the Olympic Games. Picture this pure energy going into the Earth Star chakra of the planet.
2. Many people in London and other big cities are ungrounded. They are floating over life rather than embracing it. Place the word London on an Orb of Archangel Sandalphon, so that his energy can ground this city.
3. Play a low-frequency crystal bowl or other instrument and focus on London. This will help to ground it.
4. Connect with the unicorns, the elemental Master of Air, Dom, and the air elementals, the sylphs, and ask them to blow away the lower energy in London and bring in wisdom.
5. Light a candle for London to transmute the fear that was triggered in all who heard it, when the Archbishop of Canterbury talked about the fear of God at the Royal Wedding, and focus on the unconditional love of God.

When the Earth Star chakra is open, it will enable the other fifth-dimensional chakras in the world and the Stellar Gateway in particular to awaken. London, the Earth Star, will then access wisdom and spiritual information from Sirius and the Sun to which it is connected.

Sirius is the star of the higher mind. This includes technology, especially spiritual technology for the new Golden Age and sacred geometry. Children currently incarnating from Sirius or who have stepped their energies down through that star are already programmed with spiritual technology. Because of the Earth Star's link with Sirius, many of these souls will be attracted to incarnate in London.

The Sun is the divine masculine energy source of our universe. It radiates the qualities of fairness, strength, majesty, courage and inspired leadership, so after 2012 this location will attract souls who have these qualities or who wish to develop them.

Archangel Sandalphon is in charge of the Earth Star chakra. He brings balance and a deep connection to the Earth. In addition, he is known as the Archangel of Music because he works with sound. The angels create sonics through sounds and sacred geometry and in this way touch the world. So, when this planetary fifth-dimensional chakra opens fully it will become a music centre, from which pure healing music will flow carrying the pure frequency of the angels.

However, if the Earth Star chakra does not open fully in 2012, the city will need to be cleansed and this will involve flooding in the years to come. There is a rare astrological Yod or triangle over the horoscope of the UK on 21-12-2012. This is both expansive and transformational.

The heart chakra of our planet is in Glastonbury, in the charge of Archangel Chamuel, the angel of love. As this opens fully, a welcome will radiate from here round the world and out into the universe. Situated close to here is Avebury, which used to be a main port for spacecraft from all over the universes. Its power has been cut in two by a road, but it will awaken and become whole again. Already, the surrounding areas are preparing to fulfil their old role once more.

The heart chakra in Glastonbury is linked to Andromeda and Mars---and it is not ready for 2012. Andromeda carries the energy of the higher heart, while the ascended aspect of Mars spreads the wisdom of the peaceful warrior. The heart centre is constantly cleansing energy because so many needy people go there. Please send love here, because if it is not purified, it will be cleansed by water. Together we can prevent this and make a difference.

A vast cosmic portal containing the Christ light will open in 2012 in York. It encompasses the Yorkshire Dales. It is flowing with creativity, warmth and sensitivity, and will bring light to all the industrialized towns as well as the mining areas. This portal will radiate hope and illumination, a higher way of thinking and spiritual understanding.

Those situated close by will be affected by it quite dramatically, though the energy is so gentle they will absorb it comfortably.

The United Kingdom earned considerable karma from controlling other countries during the days of the British Empire. This occurred because the decision makers were too left-brain- and masculine-orientated, acting from logic and discipline without compassion or understanding of the heart. The soul decision of the country to balance its karma from those days by allowing mass immigration has resulted in confusion, feeling overwhelmed and political misjudgements. It must be noted that the UK also learnt much about leadership, the power of ceremony and fairness during her days of Empire.

This situation will be balanced and redressed when the heart chakra opens in Glastonbury. England has lost its purpose over the last decades. Pouring energy into financial trading and war rather than into farming and wisdom has held the UK back, making the transition more difficult than it might have been.

Many low-lying areas of this country will flood during the cleansing, which will also open the hearts of the people with compassion for those affected. There will be mass movement to higher ground.

The mountains are all pure, but those in Scotland are the purest, affected by the light from the Stellar Gateway. The UK is like a jewel, which has been flawed and encrusted in dirt. Once it has been cleansed and healed, it will truly shine. By 2032, the United Kingdom will stand in its power, radiating golden strength, compassion and wisdom. It will truly have a golden heart.

Scandinavia

~ Denmark ~

Denmark is almost surrounded by ocean, which has helped to keep the energy here clear, though the karma of its warlike past needs to be cleansed. There is still sadness in the land from the time of the German occupation and a sense of mistrust in the collective consciousness. This will be dissolved by the light coming through in 2012 and this country will develop fifth-dimensional communities easily.

~ Finland ~

Finland is holding and anchoring very pure, high-frequency light. Snow and ice over the years have cleansed the land, so there is very little clearing to do.

Many evolved souls have incarnated here and are steering this country on a higher pathway. The thirty-third cosmic portal in the North Pole, which holds the strongest energy of all the portals, will affect Finland very powerfully as will Source light flowing in directly from the Stellar Gateway chakra. When the Stellar Gateway opens, the whole of Finland will become a fifth-dimensional community, so they will not need Golden Cities. This is a very special place to live.

~ Norway ~

Norway was established on land that had been purified and cleansed by the glaciers. Also, it is almost surrounded by water, which has helped to keep its frequency high. Nevertheless the Norwegians were warlike adventurers and explorers, loving the water and courageously fighting for their personal freedom and that of their country. Desire for freedom and independence has been one of the soul qualities that make this country unique.

Norway is holding and anchoring very pure high-frequency light. Many evolved souls have incarnated here and are holding Norway on a higher pathway. The thirty-third cosmic portal in the North Pole, which holds the strongest energy of all the portals, will affect Norway very powerfully as will Source light flowing in directly from the Stellar Gateway chakra. After 2032, Golden Cities will arise here.

~ *Sweden* ~

The people of Sweden have been very grounded and connected to the Earth and this has enabled them to take wise and peaceful decisions. The karma of their expansionist period has long ago been dissolved. Like the other Scandinavian countries, Sweden is holding and anchoring very pure, high-frequency light. It has been cleansed by the weather over the years. As with Finland and Norway, many evolved souls have incarnated here. The thirty-third cosmic portal in the North Pole, holding more Christ light of unconditional love than any of the other portals, will affect Sweden powerfully as will Source light flowing in directly from the Stellar Gateway chakra. After 2032, a special Golden City will arise here.

CHAPTER 6

The Middle East

An Overview

In the distant past, this entire arid area was made up of nomadic tribes of little spiritual understanding. Then, at the fall of Atlantis, the High Priest Apollo took his tribe to Mesopotamia, and eventually the Atlanteans interbred with the local people. They brought with them huge amounts of ancient knowledge, including that which has formed the basis of Western astrology today. Their wisdom underpinned the great civilization that developed in this region.

Apollo's tribe had an advanced understanding of irrigation, which transformed the dry land and made it habitable. It was this that enabled the Hanging Gardens of Babylon, one of the Seven Wonders of the Ancient World, to be built.

At the same time El Morya, currently the Master of the First Ray of Power, Will and Purpose, took his knowledge and wisdom from Atlantis to the Euphrates. He oversaw the development of their script, so that they could start keeping records for the first time – on clay tablets. He also helped to develop the Islamic faith and its art. But everything has its cycle, and eventually Mesopotamia was conquered by the Persians, then the Greeks, the Mongols, the Ottoman Empire, and the British amongst others, until the Arab Muslims took over.

There has been much bloodshed and much creative glory over the centuries. The fear and darkness of the wars and persecutions is held deep in the land and will be cleansed by nature unless enough people send in light. The countries of the Middle East are creating their own problems by being so angry and bitter. They feel they are cheated and not valued, and this is causing self-destruct. The people need to recognize that this is the consequence of ancient karma, and that they need to change their outlook to one of being happy. Otherwise, fires, earthquakes and excess heatwaves will reflect their energy back to them.

The light is rising throughout the Middle East as in the rest of the world now. As a consequence, those who have been subjugated are no longer prepared to tolerate this. Uprisings everywhere may be savagely resisted by those in control but the light will inevitably win. Where leaders are governed by illusion and their supporters follow from blind faith, we are asked to call on the fire dragons to burn away the illusion and allow them to see truth and reality. Then call on the angels to raise the frequency.

Also, within the land has been held much ancient wisdom, and when the cosmic portal of Mesopotamia opens in 2012 or thereabouts, this wisdom will be triggered again, and its influence spread across the Arab world. This will cause a spiritual awakening in the Arab countries, so that dogma will eventually be replaced by higher understanding, and women will be respected and valued.

CHAPTER 7

Forecasts for Countries of the Middle East

~ Bahrain, Kuwait, Oman, United Arab Emirates, Libya, Qatar ~

These are states rich in oil. Where there has been dictatorial rule, the people will clamour for freedom and this will cause huge upheaval and fighting. As with everywhere else on the planet, the light of freedom will eventually win.

Despite their reputation for canniness, many Arabs had childlike, innocent minds, and it was a tremendous change for them to find huge reserves of oil on their land.

These states are learning lessons similar to those individuals who win the lottery. Huge wealth demands self- and community responsibility. It raises questions, such as 'Who can you trust?' 'Who are your friends and who just wants to exploit you?' 'What do you do with all the money coming in?' 'Do you use it wisely on health, housing, welfare, education, eradication of poverty and social equality, or do you splurge it on material goods and seek the power that money brings?' 'What do you do about your family?'

They also must decide whether to extract all the oil, damage the planet and leave nothing for future generations, or whether to husband their resources, honour the planet and tread lightly on it.

In fact, these countries have all created karma for themselves. In the dance of relationships, also many other countries have earned karma for their manipulation of the oil-rich states. In places where the oil has been extracted much healing is needed, and healers are asked to send their light to Mother Earth herself here.

As with Saudi Arabia, the planet will react against the exploitation of its resources and when oil runs out and their money has no value, these states will face huge challenges. However, when the cosmic portals of Mesopotamia and the Sphinx awaken, higher wisdom will start to be activated in all these places. The spiritual throat chakra of Earth, in Luxor, Egypt, will also raise the frequency of these areas, and people will start to communicate this wisdom worldwide. They will create telepathic links with animals and once again honour water for its cosmic properties.

Development will be slow but wise old souls are already starting to incarnate in these countries, to remind people who they are and help take them forward in a higher way.

~ Bahrain ~

In early 2011, my guidance was that the monarchy feels it is doing the right thing for the people but they are out of touch. The light coming up will cause them to change and this process has already started. Many who are influenced by the mass hysteria do not want to overthrow everything, so the country needs calm for people to see the vision of freedom and fairness with or without a monarchy. This will hopefully be achieved by 2012.

~ Dubai ~

This is a country dedicated to excess, greed and materialism. The economy is not in tune with the frequency of the planet and has already started to collapse. It is difficult for people here to raise their vibrations, as they are so out of touch with the Earth. The changes ahead offer opportunities to the people to communicate, co-operate and develop qualities of patience, humanity and self-responsibility. However, a difficult transition, with much cleansing, is forecast unless there is a huge change in attitude.

~ *Iran* ~

The peoples of this vast country have tried several times to set themselves free but ancient karma has been holding them back, keeping them subjugated. The karma will be cleared by 2012, but the impact of the energy from Atlantis is felt by many here, especially as the light is rising. So things will not be fair and fine here by 2012, unless attitudes change. At present there is huge confusion and the people are lost. We are asked to call on Angels of Peace, the Archangels Uriel and Butyalil, and the cosmic angel to help the people of this country to find themselves. After 2012, when the portal in Mesopotamia, Iraq, opens, the light will profoundly affect Iran. The people will feel their souls are liberated again, and peace and joy will eventually return here.

In 2011, as I write this, a huge earthquake is forecast for Iran, which lies on a fault line. At present, the ley line is shaking as a consequence of all the fear and anger pouring down from the citizens – this is energizing the quake. A natural catastrophe can be averted if enough people send peace and light to this country. Please direct light and prayers to the Universal Angel Gersisa, who is in charge of the ley lines, to calm and soothe the energy here. Together we could change the forecast disaster into peace.

~ *Iraq* ~

Western troops will withdraw by 2012 but this is a very troubled area where turmoil will continue. Unless huge amounts of light are sent here, fires, floods and earthquakes will cleanse the land. The chaos caused by this will force the inhabitants to learn to co-operate with each other for the good of their country. Women will have to take an active part, and this will enable them to regain their self-respect and become empowered, thus bringing in the divine feminine.

The rising consciousness of women will help to loosen the grip of religious dogma, and by 2032 the people will be opening to the higher spiritual understandings pouring into the planet.

When the portal of Mesopotamia opens soon after 2012, it will start to lighten up the energy in Iraq. Then the wisdom of ancient Persia held within the land will emerge and eventually, during the next Golden Age, take Iraq to a higher level than before.

~ Israel ~

Huge cleansing is needed here, and this will predominantly take place by earthquake, though other means will be used as well. As a result, less land will be available.

However, several things will change the situation beyond recognition. The feelings of fear and vulnerability, which underlie the aggression of the Israeli people, will be dissolved as they start to become spiritual rather than religious. The old dogma will be replaced by peaceful hearts that seek resolution not conflict.

Because the United States will have problems of their own, there will no longer be support to bolster up Israel's bravado, and a new humility will change the attitude of the people from Israel.

As other countries in the Middle East suffer their own cleansing crises, the formerly conflicting countries will become helpful neighbours, looking at each other with compassion rather than fear. Israel will be at peace by 2032.

~ Libya ~

Light is rising here as elsewhere and people are no longer prepared to tolerate oppression and lack of freedom. As the light continues to rise this feeling will spread. Inevitably bullies and dictators must fall as this happens. In addition, women must claim power to enable change to take place.

While the angels grieve to see atrocities that have been going on internally here as in many other countries, change must come from within. Ultimately more effective than attack are world prayers for peace, invoking Archangel Uriel to transmute fear into courage, love and wisdom, and sending the Angels of Peace to sing over the people. Counter-aggression entrenches the dark. It is important to find a way to switch on the light quickly.

The outcome of this current war is not yet written. So the more light and prayers that we send to this country the better. Every single individual can influence the outcome.

~ *Saudi Arabia*

Ancient karma held in the earth will cause problems, so too will more recent karma as so much oil has been removed. Oil is needed for the lubrication of the planet, which will react against the exploitation of its resources.

As this country runs out of oil and money ceases to be currency, there will be challenges of self-worth and confidence when the people discover their newfound wealth is worthless.

Camels hold much wisdom, and these animals will start to communicate telepathically with the people. This will help the Saudi Arabians to find their soul path and build a country based on respect between men and women, and on an understanding of spiritual law.

CHAPTER 8

Asia

An Overview

Asia is in the charge of the angel of wisdom, Archangel Jophiel. It is a warm-hearted place, where joy and love prevails despite the challenges. There are deep connections within the communities situated there. Its people are positively affected by an ancient red-orange energy that runs deep within the ground of this continent and the areas surrounding it. It was brought from Venus thousands of years ago by beings that incarnated in Asia, and it is destined to be fully released after 2012.

This energy will ensure that everyone stays grounded and balanced as the higher force and new light comes in and also that people will remember what is truly important, so that they get their priorities right. In addition, it spreads happiness, vitality and a sense of freedom. This ancient red-orange energy is controlled by the portal of Hollow Earth.

CHAPTER 9

Forecasts for Countries of Asia

~ *Afghanistan* ~

The planetary Third Eye chakra, the all-seeing eye of enlightenment, is in Afghanistan. It is under the charge of Archangel Raphael, the angel of healing, abundance and enlightenment. This chakra is linked to the wisdom of Andromeda and Orion. The Andromeda galaxy is attuned to higher healing, which will pour through this country soon after 2032. Orion is the constellation of wisdom.

Western troops will be out of Afghanistan by 2012 but big problems will remain within the country. During the cleansing, there will be earthquakes and floods, as snow melts, and this will wake the people up.

As more people become enlightened, this will help to bring wisdom and peace to this country and by 2032 the Afghan people will be moving towards this state. When it comes into its true soul energy, Afghanistan will be amazing. Eventually, this country will play a big role in bringing the light to the whole world.

The mountains of Afghanistan have long been known for deposits of high-quality lapis lazuli, a stone that holds ancient wisdom and is connected to the Third Eye. Magnificent emeralds are also found here; they are the concretized energy of Archangel Raphael, who is bringing forward abundance, healing and the clearing of the Third Eye. Many other crystals and gems are embedded in the rocks of Afghanistan. These are maintaining the frequency of the country, so that when it finally awakens a Golden City will emerge here.

~ *India* ~

The economic situation will be an issue in India but the main challenge for the people will be flood and famine. The world will need to assist.

The planetary Soul Star chakra is located in Agra, India, and this is linked to Alcyon, the brightest star in the Pleiades cluster, which radiates healing. This chakra is in the charge of Archangel Mariel.

There are two cosmic chakras opening, which will radiate Christ light and assist the progress of this country. One is at the source of the Ganges. This is slumbering, ready to open in the very late summer of 2011 bringing with it energies from Metatron's heart and aura. It will have a big impact on the weather conditions and the earth itself in this area, and for about 5,000 miles in all directions — the further away, the less affected the place will be. The energy will clear out the old, creating a very positive, loving change and assist India to ascension.

The second is at Varanasi and this one is opening before 2012. While divine light of many colours comes through this portal, it mainly radiates rich spiritual purple. It is this that has helped to create the special bonds and unique purity that many families in this area and throughout the culture have experienced. The people are ready to be guided once more, and this will begin when they reconnect with the light emanating from this portal. It is already starting to affect the population, especially the children and psychic sensitives. Eventually it will impact very positively on everyone.

In addition, India holds a huge energy centre at Agra, on which the Taj Mahal was built. This is the Soul Star chakra of the planet and resonates with the number eleven, which means bringing in energy to start again at a higher level. When this opens in 2012, it will have a massive effect on the consciousness of the people.

Despite the opening of the cosmic portals and the Soul Star chakra, progress throughout India is forecast to be slow. However, there will be peace within the next twenty years. Currently India has lost its soul and because of this; its people have become physically and materially impoverished.

There has always been flooding in parts of India, and this will continue and be more severe as the cleansing of old energies takes place. However, when the people in India find their spiritual connection again, they will radiate an energy that will attract in abundance once more. Once this happens, women will be honoured, the caste system will dissolve, and India and its people will glow with light again.

Many souls from Sirius have incarnated in India over the last twenty years. They bring with them much technological knowledge, and minds that are open to new and higher ways of creating things. As the frequency of this country slowly rises, they will be accessing much of the higher scientific information to take the world forward. Many of these scientists will become travelling teachers, helping to spread new understandings at a time when travel will be more difficult.

There will be flooding and famine in the north of India. Also though, this part of the world holds beautiful pink energy in the land itself that will promote community spirit and love. In addition, angels will be singing over the mountains and this will greatly affect people living here.

~ *Pakistan* ~

The whole country needed cleansing, for too many power-hungry people were living here. In 2010, I was bemused that such severe flooding occurred in Pakistan long before the worldwide cleansing of the planet, forecast for 2017. Then Kumeka explained that the soul energy of these countries was so aware of the importance of being ready for the start of the new Golden Age that they petitioned to start their cleansing early. In one way, it is simply dreadful to see what has happened. In another, it is so encouraging that the souls of certain countries are taking responsibility for moving the planet forward into higher dimensions. It is triggering us all to open our hearts with compassion and enabling more people to link to the cosmic heart.

The majority of people themselves are gentle and caring, though held back by restricted cultural mores. Others are rigid and extreme. Their leaders are confused amongst themselves by the demands and pressures of other governments and the needs of their population. They need clarity and direction to find themselves.

The high-frequency energy held in the Himalayas will also assist this country. When India finds its soul, there will be an impact on Pakistan too, and by 2032 the country will be moving towards peace.

~ Tibet ~

Tibet will be free and independent from China by 2022. China will hold on as long as possible but the people will no longer want to keep Tibet in their thrall. By 2032, Tibet will once again be a beacon of light; the Tibetans, though, will no longer want to contain the light within their own country. They will be ready to spread it out to the planet.

Through forgiveness and spiritual practices, they will have cleansed the land of the darkness of the tyranny they have experienced. This is something that people all over the world can achieve if they follow the example of the Tibetans.

The planetary causal chakra is in Tibet. It is linked to the spiritual aspect of Sirius, known as Lakumay, which will be downloading sacred geometry and aspects of the higher mind to the people here. It is in the charge of Archangel Christiel.

In addition, there is a cosmic portal opening in Mesopotamia, which will affect Tibet. This portal returns to us the wisdom of Golden Atlantis that was brought here by the tribe of Apollo after the fall. When you link into it, it gives you courage, wisdom and loving self-acceptance.

CHAPTER 10

Forecasts for Countries of the Far East

~ *China* ~

By 2032, it is expected that China will have changed profoundly. The earthquake of 2008 made it possible for them to accept help from the rest of the world. It also opened the hearts of the Chinese people collectively to the families of the bereaved. Over the next twenty years there will also be massive transformation, much of it prompted by tragedy as the country is cleansed by more natural disasters.

~ *Weather* ~

The soul of China knows the importance of the huge changes ahead. Instead of waiting until the worldwide purification is set in motion in 2017, it has called its cleansing in early—hence some of the earthquakes and mudslides that have already started.

~*Economy* ~

Economically, China is in a strong position. Their financial affairs will be handled from their dogmatic position until about 2020, so that their own people do not significantly benefit. But then, people power will ensure that citizens will receive their fair share of wealth in the years to come.

~ *Spiritual Influences* ~

Because Eastern and Western cultures are so very different, the Chinese believe they are spiritual while the West is not. As the twenty-year period progresses, the West – like the rest of the world – will experience trauma, which will cause people to work together rather than in separation, driven by a desire for power and material wealth. Then the East will begin to see the West as spiritual.

The planetary base chakra is in the Gobi Desert, China. The purpose of the fifth-dimensional base chakra is to ground into the world the higher energies of bliss, wisdom and healing. Healing is particularly significant as the chakra is connected to the Pleiades, the star cluster of healing. Archangel Gabriel is in charge of this planetary chakra, and he will help to bring purification, clarity and joy through the Gobi Desert to raise the frequency of the world.

Three of the thirty-three cosmic chakras bringing in the golden Christ light of unconditional love are located in China, and they will profoundly affect this country.

One is in the mountains along the Silk Road, where Quan Yin holds the energy. This has been asleep for a long time and will be starting to open in 2012. In addition, working closely with Quan Yin here is Archangel Gersisa, the illuminated Universal Angel who is in charge of the Hollow Earth chakra, the seventh-dimensional paradise in the centre of Earth. Gersisa is grey, the perfect balance of black and white, yin and yang, masculine and feminine energy. This portal too holds grey light.

When this portal opens it will bring about deep cleansing as well as perfect harmony and balance. The energy will touch mass consciousness and help people to understand the world, to assess others correctly and to hold the fifth-dimensional vision. It will profoundly affect those who live near it or connect with it.

The second cosmic portal to open in China is Wuham in the East; it is opening gradually between 2012 and 2014. Those who travel intergalactically in their sleep to do service work will already be familiar with the energy radiating from here. They will almost certainly not be conscious of this, but when these and others who can tune into this frequency are ready, they will be able to give spectacular healings, levitate and demonstrate the physical possibilities that are available to us.

The third of the cosmic portals to open in China is in Ansi in Northern China; it is due to open in 2012. This is a portal of wisdom. Many will feel a calling to visit the place, either in their spirit body during sleep or meditation or physically. The energy will draw out the vast potential of many people and force those with active minds to contemplate the incredible wonders of creation and spirituality.

Currently there are many powerful portals and sacred sites that are not activated. As the people awaken spiritually, these places will re-ignite and the portals will open. The light coming through them will touch the hearts and open the transcendent chakras of the masses. It will have an enormous impact on the country as a whole.

A large percentage of the Chinese population will begin to see spirits and angels, so they will start to ask questions. It will be difficult for even the most diehard sceptics to deny the presence of spirit when they can see and communicate with them. This will open their right brain, their creative, intuitive, expansive and spiritual aspect, and will offer each individual the possibility of making their own personal connection with Source.

China is held back by the number of aborted souls who are stuck and have not passed over properly. As the people open up and start to communicate with these souls, they will enable them to move into spirit. This will clear the energy fields over China and raise the frequency of the country.

Once more, the divine feminine influence of Quan Yin will be felt and China, like Japan, will again understand all the elementals, especially the dragons. As a nation, their entire way of thinking about life will be transformed.

Within twenty years, the Generals will go and be replaced by a system that my guide Kumeka calls 'Community Love'. Each community will be autonomous and governed with integrity and for the highest good by the local leaders. People will feel safe. There will be much more freedom for the masses who will learn to honour the divine feminine. This will result in them respecting and honouring girls.

As the people feel more in tune with their world, safer and more trusting, they will be ready to stand up for their rights and at the same time share and co-operate with each other. They will treat all animals, especially dogs, in a more loving way, and begin to value them as evolved souls on their own pathway.

After 2032, when higher energies once more flood the planet, the Chinese people will open to their true wisdom and the vast country will be filled with light.

~ Japan ~

Japan holds karma in the land from times of cruelty and subjugation. These dark places must be cleansed, which will happen by further earthquakes in the future. These will bring people together and make them feel humble.

~ The Earthquake and Tsunami of 2011 ~

The oversoul of Japan felt the acceleration of the light and the ascension of the planet, and the souls wanted to participate fully in the move to the light. They also wanted to share their spiritual connection with dragon elementals and the divine feminine influence of Quan Yin, which they feel they have to offer to the world.

The tsunami and earthquake of 2011 was caused because of karma that was holding Japan back. This karma stems from past action in wars, including those of ancient times, from their terrible cruelty to the fifth-dimensional dolphins and whales, and their pollution of the oceans. All this needs to be cleansed, and the earthquake on the fault line and the tsunami have now started the process. The devastating tsunami, watched in horror by the world, both cleansed and destroyed. It reminded us all of the power of water and the impotence of frail humans against the forces of nature. It called on us to work with nature and to pour light into the oceans and land rather than pollute it.

The tragedy brought forward qualities such as discipline, calmness, stoicism, sacrifice, co-operation and caring, patience and endurance, which were admired by the world. Their ability to receive has also softened and changed the Japanese as a nation, to prepare them to take in more of Quan Yin's divine feminine energy. It will change their priorities. Most importantly, the tragic events induced the humility to ask for help, which will eventually propel Japan into ascension.

It is time for humans to watch and respond to the animals, who react to the vibrations of an earthquake or a tsunami before they occur. As a result of the qualities developed in the tragedy, the cleansing that was expected to happen in 2020 will now happen by 2015. Japan will be ready to help itself in the future.

~ Nuclear Power Plants ~

Japan was also drawing the attention of the world to the dangers and vulnerability of nuclear power stations. Warnings for some years about the dangerous plant were ignored here as in other parts of the world.

We have long been told that humans do not have a high-enough consciousness to handle nuclear power stations, so some disasters are inevitable. This present tragedy was calling on everyone to look at this form of power and re-evaluate. It is time to focus on natural forms of power. When writing *2012 and Beyond,* I was told that when the world was at peace and could act together in co-operation, the technology would come forward to use wave and other natural power effectively, to power the whole world without costing the Earth in any way.

Elegance, beauty and rhythm are in the collective soul of Japan. However, like China, they believe the West to be unspiritual. Their views will change as the whole world works together in the face of natural disasters. The Japanese will open their hearts and expand their consciousness to embrace a wider universe.

~ Economy ~

Economically, the double-dip recession anticipated will cause hardship to the masses. Throughout Europe and elsewhere people will be so enraged by the greed of the bankers and some big corporations that eventually it will boil over. The rigid structure of society has robbed some people of personal freedom and disempowered them. This is just beginning to change as workers express their frustration and start to claim their power.

The economic conditions along with the overall cleansing will finally break down the old structure by 2015. The old dogmas will dissolve as citizens claim their power, and economic fairness will be in place before money ceases to have value. Here as elsewhere, by 2032 food and water will be more important than cash.

~ Spiritual Influences ~

On the plus side, the Japanese have great personal discipline, which is an important part of spiritual development. It is easier to be disciplined when one is on the attack or aiming for a tangible outcome than when creating peace. So their discipline is good but the focus has been wrong. If this country had focused on peace and harmony instead of warrior qualities, it would have been truly amazing. Japan, China and much of the East had a very strong connection with dragon energy. Dragons are fourth-dimensional elementals that can help us tremendously if we are open to them. As changes take place in their world, the people in Japan will reconnect with the dragon elementals once more, and they will bring strength, protection and companionship to support communities as outmoded structures break down. This will help them to rise above their problems and open up to higher spiritual dimensions. At the same time, the divine feminine influence of Quan Yin will enfold the people, just as it did in former times and women are becoming recognized, valued, honoured and treated as equal to but different from men.

The cosmic portals at Angkor Wat, at Manila and Uluru in Australia will bring in higher spirituality when they open in 2012.

The portal at Angkor Wat, Cambodia, will help people develop friendships on a physical level and also connect with friends in spirit, including the angels. Most importantly, it will enable people to access their own ancient wisdom.

The portal in Manila, the Philippines, is very special. Archangel Gabriel works closely with this energetic space, which is a direct channel to heaven, so the energy is predominantly white. Cherubs, Seraphs and unicorns also frequently use it. It blesses those who are ready and offers grace to dissolve past karma. It helps people to feel clear, trouble-free and full of hope and happiness. The influence of this portal will bring joy to Japan.

The third portal influencing Japan is Uluru in Australia, which connects with Aboriginal wisdom. This will help to bring back an understanding and love of nature and the land.

By 2032 this country will be filled with grace and joy.

CHAPTER 11

Africa

An Overview

Archangel Uriel is in charge of Africa and of the Solar Plexus chakra of the world, which covers the whole of South Africa.

The second Golden Age, known as the Age of Petranium, took place in this continent. At that time seventh-dimensional beings connected with the land, living a deep symbiotic understanding of nature and the elements. All that wisdom and information is waiting to emerge during the transition years to 2032.

The fourth Golden Age was Lemuria, a time when the beings were etheric, like fairies or angels. Nevertheless, they positively and powerfully influenced the planet for good. Many of them were connected with the Northwest of Africa. Here, much ancient dark energy is held within the earth itself, and it is this that underlies the violence throughout the continent. The Lemurian healing energy waiting to return will eventually transmute this, for the beings of Lemuria placed their extraordinary healing crystals within the earth, energized specifically to help with the transition years. This was to ensure that Africa would be prepared for the new Golden Age starting in 2032.

Many of those Lemurians who were connected to Earth at that time have reincarnated now in physical bodies, and they are being prepared worldwide to practice Lemurian healing. This is vitally important for the world, and many of the teachers of the Diana Cooper School are facilitating Lemurian healing courses to teach those who are ready and interested to do this service work.

This means that it is from within the land in Africa that the healing and purification can now take place. It is time to programme and direct Lemurian healing crystals to purify the dark crystals in Africa, so that big changes can take place. Lemurian healing crystals need to be taken to Egypt too. Then a new grid of light can be set up, allowing Africa to take her true place in the world.

As the consciousness rises, Africans will start to demonstrate maturity and wisdom. The general frequency will rise and the people of this continent will move towards enlightenment and ascension.

This will bring healing and end the AIDS epidemic, but not until about 2032. The opening of the planetary chakra at Honolulu will powerfully accelerate this.

African people have huge, generous hearts and they will forgive the many iniquities that have been perpetrated on them over the centuries, including the blot of slavery. The Africans will understand that holding onto anger only harms you and ultimately holds the world back. They will let go and demonstrate the power of forgiveness to the world.

Africa will blossom into a land of peace and plenty. The great two-way interdimensional portal at Great Zimbabwe will wake up and become fully operational. It will bring in huge light, which will affect the country considerably. The portal of Table Mountain will also open completely, and its influence will enable Africa to become totally self-sufficient.

There are two cosmic portals opening in Africa. One is in Mali, connecting with the Dogon wisdom. The second cosmic portal is the Sphinx in Egypt. Beautiful and gentle energy pours from here, and it will help everything come into a better balance. Masters communicate with those who can hear them through this portal.

Most importantly, the whole of South Africa as the spiritual Solar Plexus chakra of the planet is currently holding fear for the world. As the portals open and are activated again, starting in 2012, the anxiety will dissolve and the ancient wisdom will return. As South Africa is connected to Mercury, the planet of communication, this country will be instrumental in spreading golden truth.

CHAPTER 12

Forecasts for Countries of Africa

~ *Egypt* ~

Archangel Metatron's retreat is at Luxor in Egypt. He is holding the ascension energy for the planet and draws great light into this country. At the fall of Atlantis, the High Priest Ra led his tribe to Egypt, so they form the basis of the Egyptian culture, bringing forward the Pharaohs. Ra's tribe brought with them the design of the Pyramids, which are awesome cosmic computers, helping to hold the Earth in alignment with the stars.

The energy of the Sphinx has been on Earth forever, and Ra also took this from Atlantis to Egypt. It is connected to Mars, protects and watches over our planet and holds the Akashic Records at a fifth-dimensional level. The ascended aspect of Mars is Nigellay, which radiates the peaceful warrior energy. When the incredible portal of the Sphinx opens, it will have a monumental impact on the Middle East and Africa, ultimately embracing the whole world.

Crystal healing grids are also being laid throughout Africa, between the Sphinx in Egypt and South Africa, to generate healing energy and bring the continent into harmony.

The planetary throat chakra is in Luxor, Egypt, which is connected to the Milky Way. It is in the charge of Archangel Michael.

As the Principal of the Diana Cooper School, I have received guidance that the school hold its annual reunion in 2011 in the Temple in Luxor, on the first cosmic moment on 11-11-11. At 11:11 am on 11-11-11, the portal here will open and energy from the centre of the Great Pyramid in Hollow Earth will come up through the portal to the four ascension planets (Neptune, the Pleiades, Orion and Sirius), and then to Source. At the same time, the energy of Source will come down through the four ascension planets to the portal at Luxor. Those standing there at 11:11 am will receive this pure Source energy and the wisdom of the ascension planets. They will link Earth into an intergalactic grid. This will assist the ascension of Earth, this universe and all the universes, and light it all up.

We were told to allow visitors to join us, and that all those called to be here will already be intergalactic masters though they will not necessarily have woken up yet. As with all spiritual service, there are rewards offered. Those who hold the energy here receive Metatron's orange cloak into their aura, which connects them with the light, wisdom and protection of Metatron and enables them to spread his energy.

If they already carry it, the gold cloak of wisdom and peace will be added. This will connect them with the angels of peace to feel true inner peace, balance and much more.

The same thing will happen at various other cosmic portals throughout the planet, though different rewards and gifts will be received.

It was forecast that at the full moons at the end of 2012, the Nile would flood in an unprecedented way, finally cleansing the fear held in the land. It is very necessary to cleanse the land here, as Egypt is very important for the future of our planet. However, the uprising of the people and the light and prayers poured into this country have changed the energy, so that floods are no longer necessary. There will be a huge shift here after 2012, and the mass of the population will open up spiritually.

~ Mali ~

After the High Priest Ra brought his tribe from Atlantis to Egypt, the Dogons, who were a part of that group, moved further down Africa and settled in Mali. They carried with them wisdom and ancient knowledge from Sirius and still hold it for us all now. The portal is expected to open in 2012. Its light will touch newborn children and ensure that they bring with them a clear pure memory of the light and wisdom.

~ *South Africa* ~

The fifth-dimensional planetary Solar Plexus chakra covers the whole of South Africa. Like your personal yellow Solar Plexus chakra, the planetary one takes in fear and transmutes it into golden wisdom. South Africa is dissolving and clearing the fear of the world, which is why it rarely shines, for more negative energy pours into it as soon as it has transmuted what it has already taken in.

Furthermore, Earth is the cosmic Solar Plexus chakra for the universe, and again we are transmuting the fear of the universe through the chakra in South Africa.

The World Cup in 2010 helped hugely to dissolve negativity, as excitement and light was focused onto the football. It brought the whole of Africa into the light.

Every living organism emits a sound. Each chakra, continent and planet resonates to a specific note. The note of the Solar Plexus is B. The note of Africa is B. The note of Earth is B. The note of the vuvuzela that was heard incessantly worldwide during the World Cup is B. It was clearing the fear drawn to the planetary Solar Plexus chakra of South Africa and helped it to shine.

South Africa is linked to Mercury, the planet of communication and will greatly help the world in the future.

CHAPTER 13

South America

An Overview

As people power is rising throughout the world, unrest is spreading. There will also be physical changes here, some of which will affect the earth, such as earthquakes and mine collapses. However, this continent has many wonderful energies and magic in it. It will offer creativity and much more to the world.

The sounds and overtones produced here by the mountains and forests vibrate through the ground and affect the whole planet.

We currently have access to only a fraction of the Mayan wisdom. When it is all available again to everyone, South America and the whole world will be enriched by it. South America will be a continent of happiness and spiritual abundance, where all countries will blossom.

~ *Economy* ~

Unlike the rest of the world, there will be no double-dip recession here and the economies will be steady. South America holds many of the answers to world economy and will inspire the world by adopting and finding solutions. This continent will wake the world up. They will find natural ways of creating enough money to survive. Through television and media, the world will see that South America is happy and will start to question their own systems and make changes.

~ *Spiritual Influences* ~

At the end of Atlantis, the kundalini or spiritual life force of the planet was taken to the Himalayas, where it was held by Sanat Kumara in his retreat in the Gobi Desert. It was a masculine energy. This energy has now been moved to South America, where it has transformed into a ball of feminine energy. Archangel Sandalphon in his retreat in the Magical Crystal Caves, at the beautiful Lake Atatlan in Guatemala, is now overseeing this energy. It will be released when the kundalini of the planet rises in 2012. Then South America will start to flower.

CHAPTER 14

Forecasts for Countries of South America

~ Brazil ~

This vast country is currently affected by the devastation of the forests, mining and corruption. However, cosmic love from Venus deep within the Earth is waiting to rise. This will raise the consciousness of the people, who will realize the importance of the trees. The people will claim their power and start caring for the land again.

There is a long tradition of healing in this country. In the recent past many of these healers have been persecuted by the Church, state and military but at last healers are finding refuge and are practicing more freely. This is expanding the consciousness of many South Americans.

~ Chile ~

In 2010, when I heard that there were miners trapped in Chile, my heart sank. Then we learnt there were thirty-three of them, and my heart leapt and I was sure they would emerge, for thirty-three is the number of the Christ consciousness, the energy of unconditional love. The fact that this took place in South America is also important, for this continent is connected with Venus, the cosmic heart, and draws in and carries the love energy for the world. The borehole went through on 10-10-10, the day of new beginnings, and this seemed so promising! And all thirty-three miners representing the Christ light emerged intact. What a wonderful omen for Chile, for South America and the world.

For the miners themselves it was an initiation – I write about initiations in *2012 and Beyond*. These are always extremely challenging and life-changing and many souls are undergoing them at this particular time, for they offer huge opportunities for spiritual growth. It was a spiritual transition for the world.

~ *Guatemala* ~

Not only has the kundalini of the planet been moved to Guatemala, but also the cosmic heart is here and is opening now. It is connected to Venus, the heart chakra of this universe.

~ *Honduras* ~

There is a cosmic portal here at the Mayan settlement, which is opening before 2012. The energy of this portal is warming, and it will melt away as much pollution as possible by influencing us to live in a spiritual way. People feel at home when connected with it.

~ *Mexico* ~

The people of Mexico hold a feeling of unworthiness and guilt within their collective consciousness and fear within the land, which is why the Unites States has resisted them so strongly. This will be cleansed soon. There is also much wisdom held within the land. Local portals are starting to awaken, affecting the people and bringing forward the ancient wisdom. In addition, when the portals of Sedona, Arizona and Hawaii open, this will profoundly affect the consciousness of Mexicans and their neighbours. By 2032, this will be a glorious place to be.

~ *Peru* ~

The planetary crown chakra is in Machu Picchu, Peru, in the charge of Archangel Jophiel, angel of wisdom. It is linked to Saturn and the Moon. Saturn is the star of order and spiritual discipline, while the moon radiates the divine feminine. Mighty great light beings gather here for it is one of the four two-way interdimensional portals on the planet.

In addition, the whole of Peru is a cosmic portal carrying the Christ light and connected with Inca wisdom, which was brought here by the High Priest Thoth at the fall of Atlantis. This portal is opening in 2012 and will help us live to our full potential. Our own energy has to vibrate at a high rate in order to do this, which can make it challenging to remain grounded. However, the Earth feels strong here and works in perfect harmony with the portal, which will help people to feel connected to the planet. Generosity is enhanced by this portal.

Lightworkers have made huge efforts to send light and protection to this portal and it is becoming clearer.

While Lima is very dark and will need to be cleansed, the Andes Mountains are a belt of pure energy. The trees that cover the area also keep the energy held as high as possible, for they contain ancient wisdom. From here, elementals send out telepathic messages of support and encouragement to their fellow elementals and the tree network.

Commander Ashtar uses the portal at Machu Picchu to access Earth with his spaceships in order to help and protect us. The angels of communication also come through here, bringing the crop circles with their symbols to wake us up. Peru will ultimately be a country of great light and compassion.

The crystal skull created by the High Priest Thoth in Atlantis will be released to its custodians in 2012, and we will all unconsciously benefit from the information programmed into it.

CHAPTER 15

Russia and Mongolia

~ Russia ~

There are six cosmic portals set to radiate Christ light throughout Russia and Mongolia, opening between 2012 and 2014.

THE FIRST PORTAL in Mongolia has a special energy for the animals, helping them wherever they are to feel happy, secure and loved. Those who connect with it fully will be able to communicate, understand and help the animals (and therefore the planet) on a completely new level. They will also find that their heart chakras open fully. Angels will work with certain people in this portal, for example scientists and some farmers, in order to help them see the world in a fifth-dimensional way. This portal will open in 2012.

THE SECOND PORTAL in Omsk, in the Urals, also opening in 2012, is extremely powerful, carrying special black and orange energy. It breaks down barriers, which makes some feel exposed. However, huge amounts of love, kindliness and generosity pour from here. This enables our Guardian Angels to connect more closely with us.

THE THIRD PORTAL is in Siberia, and many beings from other planets will use this to visit us. We can tune into it to move in and out of different dimensions. When we link with its energy, it will help us in dreams and meditation to view the past, have glimpses of the future, visit the spirit world and understand the present. Because there is so much activity here, you will automatically receive protection when you connect with it. Eventually it will affect everybody. This portal will open in 2012.

THE FOURTH PORTAL in Agata, Northern Russia, will not open fully until 2014. It holds a great deal of Christ light. This portal teaches family structure and discipline, and helps us to return to our roots, work as a team, become part of the bigger picture, and to love and accept our neighbours.

THE FIFTH PORTAL is at Opala on Kamchatka Island, Russia, also opening in 2014. This is a portal for laughter, community spirit and reality. It grounds you and helps you to know who you truly are. It enables you to understand who you have been throughout your soul journey.

THE SIXTH at Gora Chen in the Kerkeyansk Range, Russia, started to open in 2010. It holds angel light and these seventh-dimensional beings connect with us through it. The energy here ensures that you meet your fate and deal with it. Those whose vibrations are low because of unresolved emotions from this life or another will find it challenging to connect here. It can be beneficial to visit Opala first.

The opening of these major portals and others will bring in huge spiritual awakening for the people. The confidence of the masses will rise and with it their abundance consciousness, so they will attract good fortune to their countries. Currently the hearts of the people, especially the politicians, are closed with fear of the West. They need to bring the light back. This will happen by 2032, if enough individuals offer their prayers for it to do so.

The new energy coming in will open many up psychically, so that they will see things in a very different way, and it will give them hope again. The vast landmass will divide into smaller communities, who will live in harmony internally and be at peace with their neighbours.

Partly because of snow melting but for other reasons too there will be wide-scale flooding which will bring the highest out in the people. They will work hard to help their compatriots, and even open up to receive help from elsewhere.

Where the snow melts, the land will be pure, so it will attract high-frequency newcomers to create fifth-dimensional communities. Eventually, Golden Cities will arise in Russia and Mongolia, and people will laugh again.

CHAPTER 16

Australasia and
The Pacific Islands

This is one of the areas most influenced by the Lemurians during their time on the planet, before Atlantis. The Universal Angel Roquiel has his retreat over Uluru, holding the energy of Australia.

~ *Australia* ~

The economic situation will be difficult in Australia and New Zealand, though not as challenging as in Europe, America, Russia and China.

Uluru is a massive cosmic portal that will be opening soon after 2012. It connects with ancient Aboriginal wisdom, which will steadily begin to release from this portal, helping people to feel and see truth. Angels are working with the spirits of the Aborigines to take away any doubts or un-certainty we feel in our lives. The light spreading from here will help bring back an understanding and love of nature and the land.

In addition, this area will become the main welcome portal for space-ships and other beings to this universe, bringing huge benefits to this area of the world. Many star children from other planets or universes, who understand the importance of intergalactic travel and communication, will incarnate here.

When I was receiving information for my preceding book *2012 and Beyond,* I was told that initially the weather conditions in Australia would be more extreme, with unprecedented floods, heat waves and droughts, so that more of the country would become uninhabitable. Parts of Australia would disappear. Unfortunately, this has already proved to be true, with towns on the East Coast submerged.

The Queensland flooding was truly terrible, and while there will be more flooding as the transition progresses, nothing like the floods of 2011 will occur again in Australia.

As the frequency of the planet rises and scientists are allowed to 'discover' the secrets of controlling weather and creating rain, some parts of Australia will become not just habitable but pleasant and beautiful. Once the world has learnt how to bring forward the element of water and can provide it where it is needed, there will be a massive drive towards reforestation, and after 2027 Australia will change beyond recognition.

Despite the way that the English settlers treated the Aborigine natives, there is not too much karma for this country to clear. This is in part due to the way the Aborigines honoured the land for centuries, as that accumulated positive energy there.

Also, thanks to the climate many people have focused on sports and outdoor life. However, in those areas where the focus has been on the greedy accumulation of money and power, the Earth will be cleansed. This applies to all areas of the world.

The Australians will bring forward technology provided by the extraterrestrials. In accordance with fifth-dimensional principles they will share all knowledge freely throughout the world. This will be done both by distance telepathy and advanced computer knowledge that we would currently find inconceivable.

When the portal of Uluru and the portal in Hawaii containing the Great Crystal of Lemuria awaken, it will influence Australia immensely, raising the frequency and making the people gentler. They will become much more in touch with the Earth and want to heal it.

~ New Zealand ~

New Zealand's energy is pretty pristine. The people will all start to work together, co-operating for the highest good.

This area has always been an earthquake zone within the ring of fire, and the devastation of Christchurch's business centre in February 2011, which was right on a fault line, reminds us to be careful where we build and live. It was sending a call to all those living on fault lines that they are vulnerable. However, as has happened since time began, certain souls are drawn to live 'on the edge' and this will continue. This particular earthquake also warned people everywhere, that the best way to ensure the safety of any area is to live and work in the fifth dimension.

There will continue to be earthquakes here along the fault lines. This is because the land of ancient Lemuria within the ring of fire is rising again over the next few thousand years, and this will impact on the land in New Zealand. It may feel challenging, but this country will have a relatively easy passage. The areas away from the fault lines will be safe.

At the fall of Atlantis, one of the twelve tribes led by the High Priestess Hera went to the Pacific Islands and then on to New Zealand. They became the Maori, bringing with them mystical and shamanic wisdom as well as unique farming knowledge. After 2012, this knowledge will return to the consciousness of the people and help them with the future.

As more people become psychic, they will be aware that this country is already an entry portal for spaceships of light, especially those of Commander Ashtar's command, which enter here. They will embrace and welcome the presence of light beings from other planets and the help they bring.

As a result of the extrastellar assistance, New Zealand will prosper and be an example to the world, especially after the cleansing during which the supervolcano is expected to erupt.

~ *Fiji* ~

The navel chakra can be found in Fiji, and it is opening to a fifth-dimensional frequency to bring trust and friendship to the world. Harmony will spread from here to accelerate a feeling of brotherhood and sisterhood, with mutual respect for different cultures. By 2032, everyone will honour their neighbours.

A huge cosmic portal containing the Christ light will open in 2012, and is filled with ancient Maori wisdom. At the fall of their continent, the Atlanteans came to Fiji, before they continued to New Zealand. This portal balances energies allowing for the best to shine from the people and the planet. Lost memories will return and old bonds between friends and family will be re-cemented whether or not the person is in spirit or body. People will feel inspiration, understanding and oneness when they are affected by this portal.

~ *Honolulu* ~

The sacral chakra of our planet is in Honolulu. Archangel Gabriel is bringing through the fifth-dimensional pale pink energy of higher sexuality. The light spreading through here will help people worldwide raise their frequency from lust and neediness to love and caring with self-worth. As the feeling and understanding of pure sexuality radiates from this chakra across the globe, sexually transmitted diseases will start to wane and disappear totally by 2032. A knowing of transcendent sexuality will return.

~ *The Pacific Islands* ~

Fiji and Honolulu are the spiritual navel and sacral chakras of the planet in the charge of Archangel Gabriel, which is why these islands express sensuality, warmth and welcome. Both fifth-dimensional chakras in the Pacific will open in 2012.

These planetary chakras in the Pacific are connected to our own planet, Earth, so the incredible wisdom of all our ancient civilizations, portals, kingdoms and the golden ages will be spread through here. In addition, when the cosmic portal opens on Fiji in 2012, the Pacific as a whole will start to radiate pure love and spread it everywhere.

The cosmic portal of Mu, also situated in the Pacific Ocean, will open in 2012 and re-awaken the latent wisdom of the ancient civilization of Mu, which was the Golden Age prior to Atlantis and Lemuria. This energy will help others accept themselves and reach inner peace, so they can permanently leave behind the old. They can then really get in touch with who they are, and this will allow them to evolve. This portal is full of healing energy that will help to settle the weather in this area.

CHAPTER 17

Arctic, Antarctic, Canada

~ The Arctic ~

The planetary Stellar Gateway is in the pure snow-covered Arctic, which has been prepared for centuries to hold this high frequency. This place is linked to an energy cluster in the Pleiades, which connects to a wormhole that accesses Source. Archangel Metatron is in charge of the Stellar Gateway.

In addition, the cosmic portal at the North Pole is beginning to open now. The highest and purest light, including more of the Christ light than any other cosmic portal, will pour in here when the great portal of the Arctic opens in 2012. It is extremely expansive and so huge that it will influence the entire world.

All types of energies merge here and work harmoniously and positively. If you visit this portal, it will absorb and dissolve lower or harmful vibrations if this is for the higher good.

The cosmic portal in Alaska, Arctic, connecting with Inuit wisdom is also opening in 2012. This portal helps to materialize the words of the angels. It has a cleansing energy and elementals work with its light; particularly active are esaks whose task is to cleanse negativity on the planet. When you link into it, it connects you with other worlds, so you can communicate with and help them. It is a very magical place, which does not impact on the climate in any way.

This area has been covered in snow and ice for a long time, and has therefore been purified. The Inuit living here originated from Golden

Atlantis and they hold the wisdom of their tribe from that special era. Because Alaska is a high-frequency area, it will attract evolved people who will migrate here when it eventually becomes habitable, so that they can bring forward the blueprint for the fifth-dimensional world.

~ *The Antarctic* ~

The Antarctic is totally pure. As 2012 approaches, its energy will transform to help the animals of the world adapt more easily to change. The cosmic portal here is linked to the one in Yorkshire, UK, and the latter is influencing the change. Archangel Sandalphon is working in the Antarctic to spread calm and tranquility to the rest of the Earth. This is already starting to happen. This cosmic portal is connected to space and to other portals, which are outside our solar system. As a result, we will receive great help and the wisdom we absorb will be spread from here across our planet. Earth herself can benefit from being open to the energy of other planets, which can be accessed through this portal. Ultimately, this will enlighten us and enable us to see more clearly.

The cosmic portal at the South Pole is opening in 2012 and it feels full of life. It energizes and brings creativity, light and laughter to people and animals. When connecting with it, you will be able to feel your loved ones in spirit as well as the spirit world as a whole much more clearly. When linking with this portal correctly, you will be filled with bliss. After 2012, once all the portals are open and active, this one will cleanse the planet and expand our consciousness.

~ *Canada* ~

Archangel Michael's retreat is at Lake Louise, Banff, and he has been holding the energy of Canada, giving the inhabitants much strength, courage and protection. With little karma and many older souls incarnating here, this country has been cleansed by ice and snow over a long period of time. The transition years here will be relatively easy, and then its light will truly shine and also help its neighbour, America, to move into ascension.

There is a cosmic portal in Banff, Canada. This particular portal is ever-changing its size and energy. It will open in 2012, when the people are ready to hear its messages. Archangel Michael's light is very strong here, and special, sacred energy flows within the portal, which will soon spread across the world.

CHAPTER 18

USA

An Overview

America is enormous and each of the fifty states of the USA, including Alaska and Hawaii, is affected by different conditions. As weather, political and historical background of each area varies, I offer a specific sound bite for each individual state.

The whole country has been influenced by Barak Obama who has become the 44th President of the United States. His election in November 2008 created a wave of excitement throughout the world that pushed the Earth onto her ascension pathway. Forty-four is the number that vibrates with the Golden Age of Atlantis, and in that Age, Barack Obama was indeed a priest who was trained specifically to be a bridge between races, opposing sides, states and countries for his current incarnation. He came in with the qualities to take the United States forward but opposing forces such as the gun lobby, the third-dimensional dogmatic souls in the Bible Belt and the backlog of karma throughout the country have drained his resolution and power. He has felt forced to engage with lower energies rather than shine the light. It was hoped by the spiritual realms that he would be able to hold enough power to make changes, but he is not connected to the angels. In addition, his focus was intended to be on the United States, but his desire to be a world leader has meant that he is in danger of failing in his soul mission.

The karma and resistance to change will need to be cleansed and transmuted in this country. Some of this will be cleared by nature. In some areas, however, extraordinary angelic grace will help the places and people shift to a higher dimension.

At the fall of Atlantis, the High Priest Imhotep led his tribe to North America, where they settled, intermingling peacefully with the local people and spreading their great wisdom about the land, nature and the honouring of animals. Gradually, the Atlanteans lost their benign influence and the different tribes became warlike, starting to fight each other. Deep pain was left in the ground where this happened. Rage is locked into the Earth at the sites of battles, massacres and war, sadness where there was mass movement of tribes. In the slave states, many still need to understand oneness, open their hearts or learn to forgive. Throughout the continent, there has been much accrued karma over the last four hundred years, which must be balanced by 2032.

In contrast to this, the noble ideals of the Bill of Rights has given Americans a sense of freedom, justice and worth. Some highly idealistic and evolved people have incarnated here to hold the flame of independence and freedom for the world. Parts of the land are exceptionally beautiful and this beauty is reflected in the souls of many of those who live there. This has drawn in the help of the angels.

~ Weather ~

Because the continent is so enormous, the weather varies throughout. In general terms, though, it will become more severe. Cleansing will take place almost everywhere, and there will be mass movement to high ground.

~ Economy ~

Many souls are attracted to incarnate or live in the US to experience power, money, control or success. However, as in Europe, fury with bankers will erupt and the majority will realize that greed and hedonism are not the best visions. This country will be badly hit by the double-dip recession, and the citizens will start to realize they have to live in a different way, working together and supporting each other. They will start to care for each other in communities.

The flooding of New Orleans was the forerunner to cleanse the land and demonstrate the lessons to be learnt. If they are not absorbed and changes in consciousness made, continuing big natural disasters will draw attention to the huge divide between rich and poor. In that case, within the next ten years the people themselves will demand that this be redressed. Social conscience will ensure the poor receive the material help they need as well as assistance to regain their confidence and self-worth.

There will be a crisis of confidence in the country, as they realize they cannot afford to pay for oil. The oil in the Bakken oil fields and others is for the lubrication of the tectonic plates. However, the soul of America does not recognize this. It is anticipated that they will try to exploit these oil reserves, and if they do, the consequent karma will be severe in the form of major accidents and economic loss.

Another big economic hit will occur when the San Andreas fault goes, and this may well happen before 2032, unless huge amounts of light are poured into the land here.

~ Spiritual Influences ~

The Americans have a deeply entrenched belief that they are special, and even the chosen ones. As a result, they have withdrawn themselves from the rest of the world and become isolated. The cleansing that takes place here through natural disasters will cause them to ask for help. This development of humility will be the catalyst that takes this country into a higher consciousness.

The light is rising everywhere, and there are pockets of pure angelic energy in the US that will wake up the vast mass of people psychically as well as spiritually. Many will be shocked when they start to see spirits and angels, dashing their firmly held beliefs. As they start to question their beliefs, this country will be transformed from a religious one to a spiritual one. The US will ultimately become an open, caring fifth-dimensional nation.

Many people will move from places that are being purified to higher ground. The mountains everywhere will become popular places to live. As huge numbers move to the high-frequency places, their own consciousness will automatically rise.

There are six cosmic portals opening in the United States that bring in the Christ light of unconditional love, the twelve rays and the silver ray of the divine feminine.

THE FIRST ONE is the cosmic portal of Atlantis in the Atlantic Ocean. This portal is already opening, waking up the energy of the Temple of Poseidon in the Atlantic Ocean and bringing forward the wisdom of Atlantis. This will physically help people and animals alike to ascend by working with their energies and triggering their ancient gifts and talents. It will enable many to see everything in a new light and to feel more inspired, energized and knowledgeable.

THE SECOND COSMIC PORTAL, the portal of Lemuria, is based in Hawaii and also already opening. It is thereby activating the great crystal of Lemuria and returning the wisdom it holds to the Earth. This is bringing a new humility to the world, as well as a deep love of nature and a desire to heal the planet.

THE THIRD COSMIC PORTAL is called Hollow Earth because it is one of the main entry points for human energy into the seventh-dimensional centre of our planet. The opening of this portal to the centre of the Earth, happening now is affecting the ley lines. It covers Oklahoma, Kansas, Nebraska, South Dakota and the bottom of North Dakota in an oval shape. In 2012, the energy is going to be strong enough to start to return it to its original circular shape, impacting the people and the land. By 2035, it will be fully open for three years and then close slowly. The impact will be both physical and energetic; it will swiftly reform many parts of our society. Higher angelic energy will pour from it bringing compassion and love beyond that which we have yet experienced. The weather here may be a little unsettled at first, after 2012.

THE FOURTH COSMIC PORTAL is in Sedona, and this is connecting with Native American wisdom. It is opening in 2012. People influenced by this portal will start to accept their magnificent gifts and talents. Communities will stand together and begin to understand their land, their heritage, their past and their place in the world. They will know how to unlock the best from the planet, so that it can replenish itself and all can work in harmony. This portal is helping to bring about oneness. This will involve changes, but when the time is right, truth and peace will prevail.

THE FIFTH COSMIC PORTAL is a very important one in the Bermuda triangle, which houses the Great Crystal of Atlantis. The Great Crystal was held within the Temple of Poseidon and had many roles, one of which was to be a portal. When Atlantis fell, the crystal lodged at the bottom of the ocean in the middle of the Bermuda Triangle. When the Intergalactic Council needs to use the portal, it is opened and everyone and everything within the Bermuda Triangle goes through a rapid inter-dimensional shift. To human eyes, it seems that they tragically disappear, but at a soul level anyone involved agrees to this experience. They ascend to another place, ready for the next step in their evolution. The energy around this portal is thick, to protect the rest of the world from its unique and wonderful influence, which is why it will not dramatically affect weather conditions too far away from its base. The great Universal Angel Joules is in charge of this portal and the oceans.

THE SIXTH COSMIC PORTAL is in Alaska. This cosmic portal carries huge amounts of the Christ light, the golden energy of unconditional love. The high-frequency energy pouring through here will affect the whole country considerably.

In addition, Yellowstone is a huge portal for nature. The volcano here will not erupt during the transition years. Another vast portal is the Grand Canyon that holds the energy of the Pleiades, thus bringing in healing for the continent and the world.

CHAPTER 19

Forecasts for the States of America

~ *Alabama* ~

Alabama was the home to many noble Native American tribes, including the Cherokee and the Choctaw. Though they were forced to leave their lands and moved to reservations in Oklahoma and Texas, their distress remains here. So too does their spirituality. This state was deeply enmeshed in slavery and racial intolerance still abounds. As a result there is much karma to repay and cleanse, mostly by air and water, so please send bubbles of love and peace here.

~ *Alaska* ~

The land here is very pure as much of it has been under snow and ice for a long time. This area has been occupied by the Inuit who originate from the tribe the High Priest Seth led here after the fall of Atlantis, and they have been holding their ancient wisdom in this region in trust for the world. In addition, there is a cosmic portal in Alaska, which will bring the Christ light into the state and raise the frequency even higher in the surrounding areas. When the planetary Stellar Gateway chakra opens in 2012, Source light will pour into this state, turning it into a blazing light for the whole world.

~ *Arizona* ~

This state was under water for aeons, and shells and fish fossils can still be found in the desert. During that period, the land was cleansed. Later it was home to a great many Native American tribes, who revered the land and held it sacred. Unfortunately, they also fought many battles and there were massacres here, the energy of which is currently being cleansed by beings from the Pleiades.

The awesome Grand Canyon is a high-energy spot and portal in its own right, holding light for this area. When the great cosmic portal of Sedona opens in 2012, this will ignite the consciousness of the people here, bring back the Native American wisdom and remind them to love and nurture the Earth and all animals. This knowing will spread into other states. Arizona will have a relatively easy transition.

~ *Arkansas* ~

This area has at times witnessed acts of greed and manipulation, especially because of the diamond mines. Diamonds are the concretized form of Archangel Gabriel's energy and he has a great influence here. 2012 will begin to bring balance back, so that those who share the land have an equal say. Those who have lived or worked in the area for a long time will have learned many lessons – how to compromise, negotiate, feel what is right, honour the Earth and much more. The diamond mines are a high-frequency space that is collecting all the different energies of humans and animals to create data, which will act as a guide to help others worldwide to communicate, share and work together effectively.

The area does need cleansing, but not until just before 2012. Then Archangel Gabriel will do this by touching the land with his energy in a number of ways, including tornadoes and floods. People will work together to deal with the consequences, and this will help them open their hearts.

~ California ~

There are many varying influences on this state. Where there is greed and hedonism, there will be cleansing. Already, forest fires are burning away old negativity. There will also be flooding, and when the San Andreas Fault is activated, much chaos will arise, bringing out the best in people.

There are also pockets of purity in the high-lying areas, and many will retreat here. One example is Mount Shasta in the north, which is under the guidance of Archangel Gabriel and brings in healing from the Pleiades. This sacred mountain and its environs vibrate at a very high frequency. People are drawn to it but not everyone can cope with the high energy.

Commander Ashtar's spaceships come in here and connect with a number of people, who are bringing forward the extraterrestrial wisdom. This will happen more as the planet moves through its transition.

This state will be affected by the opening of the cosmic portals of Sedona, Hollow Earth and Hawaii. Those who are highly evolved will blossom as they awaken to the ancient wisdom available from these portals. They will also work together to support those in need, especially those who find it very difficult to cope with the light pouring in.

The film industry will be inspired to bring forward spiritual films in response to the hunger for spiritual information and inspiration that will arise.

~ Colorado ~

As in all mountainous areas, the land is relatively pure here. Native Americans still honour the Earth and keep the frequency light, and highly evolved people tend to gravitate here. The opening of the portal of Hollow Earth will powerfully influence this place. The mountainous areas of this state will shine in the New Golden Age.

~ *Connecticut* ~

This state holds a large amount of healing energy and pure light. This is because a portal in South Glastonbury, Connecticut, is connected with a very sacred place, full of love and light, in the seventh dimension or seventh heaven. This portal (though not a cosmic one containing Christ light) is already awake and will open fully in 2012. When you are here, you are filled with unconditional acceptance and love for all. It helps you feel happy and holy. The spirits of many who passed over in the World Wars have sent their forgiveness and tears to this place to raise its light. They will draw the world's attention here in the future, to help us all open our eyes more.

~ *Delaware* ~

Delaware has become very industrialized and is greatly affected by this. Many people and materials have come through here, all mixing their energies. Some of it is light because many people are generous-hearted, but much of it is not. Over the coming years, many factories will change or be abandoned. The area is due to be cleansed by changes in the tectonic structure, which will occur below ground. Only something this dramatic, primarily underneath the surface, will unlock the blocked energy. After the cleansing, people will be able to open their hearts, show their inner beauty and spread positive light.

~ *Florida* ~

Parts of Florida lie so low that flooding is inevitable, and this will wash away the negativity of the past, including that of slavery, war and dogma. Hurricanes too will cleanse old karma.

Places of entertainment, offering pure, innocent fun and laughter, such as Disney World, have lit up and healed other areas of Florida. They have spread lighter energy into the surrounding land, which has balanced the energy of greed.

Florida will be considerably influenced by the cosmic portal of the Bermuda Triangle, which contains the Great Crystal of Atlantis. This will enable what remains of this state to become a fifth-dimensional beacon of light to illuminate the Unites States and the world and open the people to true spirituality.

~ *Georgia* ~

This area has already begun to be cleansed. It is covered by a huge rainbow of light that is helping people and animals to feel good about themselves exactly as they are. This will enable them to be totally at one with themselves and to feel free. Then their souls will lift and soar.

The light enables those who are consumed by material desires to let them go. This will mainly affect the teenagers, who will have much influence on the planet as they become adults. It will be easy to see the changes within them, for their souls have in many ways been untarnished. In the past, some of the children living here have been overly boisterous/self-aware and done what they thought was right, no matter what the consequences. They have left traces of courageous energy, which will positively impact the teenagers now and enable them to step forward with strength and self-worth.

~ *Hawaii* ~

At the fall of Atlantis, the High Priest Hermes took his tribe to Hawaii, where they became the Kahunas. They brought the powerful dolphin link with them and much ancient knowledge associated with this. There is special energy in Hawaii, for it holds wisdom from Lemuria as well as Atlantis. The cosmic portal is opening in 2012 and, as the Great Crystal of Lemuria is held here, it will spread Lemurian wisdom and healing like rays of light round the world.

In spring 2011, Japan was hit by a massive tsunami, which sent 4 ft waves to Hawaii. This is such a special place that the tsunami brought a particular message from spirit about trust. Trust that they will always receive the guidance and advance notice they need. Trust that water is their friend. For the latter, they were reminded to work with the water elementals, like the mermaids and undines. The tsunami wave would have been less severe and they could have prevented it from hitting the island if they had done so.

~ Idaho ~

Adjacent to the cosmic portal of Hollow Earth, this state will be affected by the land changes there. There is a great deal of strength held in the land, which cannot emerge, though, until 2012. Many of the lower emotions will start to be dissolved then, and the people will honour and appreciate the land and animals, so that this area can transit into a higher dimension.

~ Illinois ~

In order for the people of Illinois to evolve in 2012, they must forget and forgive the past. This will prepare them to ascend easily, which will bring light, joy and happiness into the area. Illinois is profoundly affected by an ancient energy of magic, romance, beauty and integrity from the planet Venus. When enough people are ready, they will receive this light and will glow.

~ Indiana ~

The state of Indiana holds a special light, which is subtle, almost transparent golden-yellow, pale at the centre and darker at the borders. This particular location was chosen to hold a special quality, for it aligns with the spirit world as a result of past happenings and because of underlying energy here.

This golden-yellow light promotes friendship and teamwork, and will eventually extend from here across the world. Many of the people and animals will experience tingling on their skin by 2012, as they open up to the presence of elementals and unicorns. Indiana will be a highly spiritual area that will send light to help other places during the transition.

~ Iowa ~

This state lies to the east of the cosmic portal of Hollow Earth. It will be profoundly affected by the energetic shifts there during the next twenty years and to a lesser extent by the physical earth movements. Where there is dogma, it will be transformed into spirituality. As hearts open, attitudes to cattle, chickens and other creatures will change, and they will be treated with respect. Those living in agricultural areas will gradually become aware of the damage done by toxic sprays and fertilizers and the land will be purified. There is much light held within the Earth itself, which will help with the necessary cleansing.

~ Kansas ~

There is much fear, anger and sadness held in the land here as a result of the Indian Removal, which is waiting to be healed. Kansas is directly affected by the opening of the cosmic portal of Hollow Earth, which will bring in the force of Source as well as the Christ light, and this will profoundly touch the hearts and minds of the people in this state. It will heal the old karma and raise a beautiful loving light.

The land is heavily affected by the surrounding areas, since so many different energies merge here. After 2012, people will collaborate properly and spread joy and happiness.

~ Kentucky ~

Aeons ago, many men were conscripted to go to sea from this inland state. They were greatly affected by what happened to them at sea and by the legends they heard there. This trauma they took back home with them. It is still held within the earth. There is a portal here through which green turquoise energy is pouring to heal these feelings.

In 2012, another high-frequency, advanced healing energy will be brought to Kentucky through other portals; this will be used by those who have the humility to accept it graciously. It will be used only for the greater good of those who deserve it, and it cannot be controlled. Then the land will be cleansed enabling Kentucky to have an easy transition. Note that when anyone thinks positively about the sea, their thoughts light up the water and all the creatures in it.

~ Louisiana ~

The whole world watched the start of the cleansing in New Orleans, which drew attention to the racial and economic divides still remaining. Many thousands of years ago a group of Atlanteans came to this area, because they suspected that Atlantis would fall. These people have never reincarnated but they arrived to prepare the land for 2012, knowing that it was the end of the cosmic era and that much intolerance and injustice would occur in this region. They brought special yellow energy with them, which they planted deep into the ground; this will help people here to let go of the past and of all judgment, before it is too late for change. This is why New Orleans emanates a strong light.

There is a special magical quality waiting to arise in Louisiana, which has been hidden and unsuspected within the Earth itself. When it appears, people will realize that there is more to life than they can see. Those who can already sense and see other dimensions and worlds, will start to understand them more. This will help to dissolve the karma and pain of slavery locked into the land.

~ Maine ~

Many left-brain people who have been trained in the universities of light in Sirius and its ascended aspect Lakumay will move to Maine. These are precise, highly intellectual thinkers, and they will gather here to bring forward spiritual knowledge. They will also access and download new technology and mathematics to carry the world forward into the new Golden Age. Their clarity and focus will create an energy force that cannot easily be penetrated by those of lower frequency. This will ensure that the high-vibration information and technology they bring forward for the use of the planet will be made available to all. There will also be a spiritual protective influence as beings from Nigellay, the ascended aspect of Mars carrying the peaceful warrior energy, are drawn to this state. The spread of this energy is being watched over and protected by Archangel Gersisa, who works in Hollow Earth.

~ *Maryland* ~

Maryland is a special and important place, which is clear and pure. The whole area is heavily protected by angels who are shining light onto it. The state holds two portals: the first one on Earth is connected to the angelic world. This links to the second portal in space that is full of cosmic love. This space portal collects information about everything that has ever happened and is likely to happen in the future. It then sends energy to the planet through the first portal to help us all.

Currently this state is undergoing a dimensional shift. Sometimes it is in the third dimension. At other times, it raises its frequency into the higher ones and then happiness and warmth is felt here. Because of this fluctuating energy, it may at times seem unsettled here. In 2012, the angels are going to send down a large beam of navy blue energy, which will force all this information out to the rest of the world, and this will enable people to understand more about the planet.

~ *Massachusetts* ~

This state is mostly fifth-dimensional. Those who will be here in 2012 are very pure souls who understand how to live in harmony. This is a place of reflection, for the people hold keys to evolution. The angels sing in this area and their voices can always be heard in times of need to heal, help and give hope. After 2012, this will be a place of refuge because of environmental changes in nearby states.

~ *Michigan* ~

This state is bordered by lakes, and the proximity of the water has a purifying effect on the land. Michigan people's attitudes to the land and animals will transform in the coming years. Those who have been connected with the pure teachings of Jesus, whether they are in spirit or in a physical body, will teach others by the way they live their lives. The water will enhance their energy and amplify their message.

~ Minnesota ~

The angels will be working with children in the schools here to help them break free of old ways that have been affecting people for a very long time. By doing this, they will enable the children to ascend into the fifth dimension, but it will take a little longer for some in this area because of the dogma they have been exposed to.

~ Mississippi ~

This area is still affected by the world's fear of witchcraft over the years and by the slavery that took place here. Many of the African slaves had an inner peace that came from their humility, though they did not always show this. However, the peace they held in their energy fields was cleansing for the area as long as it lasted – but more was needed.

The slaves were also very afraid, and this prevented them and other people in the area from showing their true feelings. This fear affected everyone who came here. The fear will be dissolved, so that it no longer affects the area, its people and visitors. Those who have ever been here have experienced the fear and learnt from it. Because of this, they will find themselves more inclined to speak from their hearts and live in harmony with everyone. They will have a deeper understanding of how to bring beauty and light to all.

Where Native Americans were forced to leave Mississippi and other states, the heartbreak of the enforced separation from their homeland is still held in the aura of the area. This underlies much of the anger, which has caused racial tension in this region. When the karma is cleared by 2022, this state will be a happy place where brotherhood and sisterhood prevail.

~ Missouri ~

The minds of many people in Missouri have been closed by dogmatic beliefs, which have held the people back. They will be shocked when the higher light enters and wakes them up to other dimensions and understandings. However, the etheric retreat of Archangel Chamuel, the angel of love, is in St. Louis, Missouri, and higher light will increasingly radiate from there. This will help Missouri and spread to the other states. As the karma is cleansed, people's hearts will open, and then this will become a truly beautiful place, full of tolerance and love.

~ Montana ~

Lying to the west of the cosmic portal of Hollow Earth, this state will be profoundly affected by the energetic shifts here during the next twenty years. Montana holds the golden ray of Christ already. The Christ light is a huge energy of unconditional love which is held in the cosmos. It was brought to Earth 2,000 years ago and in recent years, more has flooded in. The light sent from Montana daily purifies the world in small amounts. This will be a high-frequency area to live in.

~ Nebraska ~

The cosmic portal of Hollow Earth encompasses Nebraska, which will be directly affected by it. In 2012, a deep red-pink loving energy will start to spread from the heart of this state across the whole world. This will encourage sweetness in people – kindness, calmness and purity, dissolving the old. It will also assist the residents of this state to handle the Earth changes during the transition period and clear old karma.

~ Nevada ~

This state contains mostly arid desert and mountains. Mountains maintain a high frequency of light, and those in Nevada are managing to hold the energy.

As this state houses Las Vegas and a nuclear test site, extreme conditions and much cleansing will take place, unless light is focused here to dissolve the old.

~ New Hampshire ~

Because of changing climate worldwide, the lower regions of this state will become greener and wetter. Some of the ice in the mountains will melt, causing this slight change in the weather and ecology. The subtle shift will raise the energy in the entire area. The trees in New Hampshire are very old and wise, and they hold the state in a high frequency. Many elementals access America through New Hampshire, and they bring light, joyful, cleansing and purifying energy with them, which is felt by everyone who passes through here. This will be a happy place to live in.

~ New Jersey ~

This is a clean state without karma and the energy is mostly very light here. People are drawn into the purity of the place, if they need to think clearly or feel relaxed. There is a one-way portal here, which takes energy from Earth to the spirit world. Within it reside many elementals, especially esaks whose task is to cleanse. The environment brings fun and positivity to the area, so there will be a smooth transition.

~ New Mexico ~

This state contains much Native American wisdom. The mountainous areas hold good clear energy, and where there is snow they have been purified. Many older souls have been attracted to New Mexico. They have been healing the legacy of ancient battles, so that the transition will be eased. Pure blue light is starting to pour from the land, and this will assist with healing and communication during the transition.

~ New York ~

New York is a mix of dark and light, fear and excitement, hope and expectation, corruption and greed. The events of 9/11 expanded the minds of many in the US. It opened hearts with compassion, and it also forced the people to ask questions, especially about conditions in poor countries.

Within the city itself, as in cities all over the world, citizens, especially those living in high-rise apartments, have lost their connection with the Earth. It is important that people start to make contact with the land and listen to their inner wisdom again. If enough did so, it would make a tremendous difference and help to light up New York.

As money ceases to have relevance towards the end of the transition, the focus of Wall Street will have changed in line with fifth-dimensional energy. Those in the third dimension whose whole sense of being and worth is about money will find this challenging to bear. But by that time, many will have raised their frequency and will be seeking soul satisfaction rather than financial reward. By 2032, New York City as we know it now will no longer exist.

Much karma has been held within the land, partly cleansed by rain and snow. However, there is more that needs to be dissolved. At the same time, ancient wisdom was placed in the land by the Native American Indians, soon after the High Priest Imhotem's tribe had arrived from Atlantis. This will be revealed after 2012, and people who feel it will want to live close to the Earth again, honouring nature.

Many people here are only focused on their work and have no connection with the place or the land. After 2012, their hearts will open and they will want to return home or connect with the love in the land here.

~ *North Carolina* ~

This area needs cleansing and is likely to be affected by flooding. However, the people who live here are well-equipped to deal with such an eventuality, spiritually as well as practically. Many have a deeply-ingrained positivity that will enable them to teach, learn, adapt and spread light.

By 2012, there will be many very happy, fifth-dimensional people here, who can enjoy what life offers rather than the material. Those who remain materialistic will be healed and helped. The angels will work closely with this area, so will the elementals, who will assist people on a one-to-one basis. They will enable their charges to evolve as a result of their experiences.

~ *North Dakota* ~

This state is deeply affected by the cosmic portal of Hollow Earth, which is bringing in the light of the twelve rays, the divine feminine and the Christ light. The energy of love and truth from this portal will flow everywhere, dissolving the old and helping people to fulfil their destinies.

Many of those who have lived here in the past learnt their lessons and have now reincarnated in other parts of the world. In the future, they will offer their expertise to help this area, especially with regard to working positively with nature. Many are sending blessings to this part of the world. There will be big challenges and earth shifts, but North Dakota will eventually radiate light to the planet.

~ *Ohio* ~

This state is being described by the angels as 'The Little Star'. Within this ground are special crystals that are connected to the energy of the Golden Age of Atlantis and the higher spiritual realms. The crystals draw in this positive energy and, when help is needed, shine it very brightly across the world. They are already active and will be responsible for a large energy cleansing around 2012, which will raise the consciousness of the people here and the vibrations on Earth. This will open everyone up to enlightenment, preparing them to move to a higher dimension.

Those who have always protected themselves by holding back their emotions will not be able to do so any longer. They will find themselves opening up and connecting to others. This is a dramatic step in the evolution of humanity as a whole and will occur around the year of 2014.

~ *Oklahoma* ~

Much fear, anger and sadness is held in the land as a result of the Indian Removal, and this must be healed. The dogma currently preached and practiced here will expand into higher consciousness under the influence of the divine feminine, as it becomes stronger. And yet, this is the state of love, compassion and understanding. Wise beings travelled here a very long time ago and shared their knowledge of love with all. This is what is to be released in the lead up to 2012. In addition, this state will be directly affected by the opening of the cosmic portal of Hollow Earth, which will bring in Source light as well as the Christ light. This will profoundly touch the hearts and minds of the people in Oklahoma, allowing them to deal with deep issues in their hearts. It will enable people to connect with their past lives, so they will remember a lot more of the ancient knowledge and wisdom held within their souls.

The cosmic portal of Sedona will also influence this area, bringing with it a deep love and honouring of the land. There will be Earth changes as well as spiritual shifts over the next twenty years. Though many will move to the mountains, by 2035, this will be a very high-frequency area to live in.

~ Oregon ~

This state is under the influence of Archangel Michael and the cosmic portal opening in Banff, Canada. It will also be touched by Archangel Gabriel whose retreat can be found in Mount Shasta in the Rockies.

Many evolved people have automatically gathered in the mountains and are holding the energy high. As a result, Oregon will flow into the fifth dimension and ascension. Later, people will flock here from the lower areas to be embraced into the higher light.

~ Pennsylvania ~

There are two energies in Pennsylvania that will profoundly affect the transition. Most of the permanent residents are holding a blue energy from the Pleiades, which will soon awaken and change their perspective on life and the world. It will lighten them up and enable them to teach, heal and live in a higher dimension. There are others who hold a different, peaceful warrior energy that is orange-pink, from Nigellay, the higher aspect of Mars. This energy is fiery and can make them very strong. It enables them to stick to their beliefs and be untouched by temptation. They will begin to soften somewhat as 2012 approaches. The dogma of their beliefs has restrained them, but after 2012 their true soul energy will shine forth. Then the people of both colour groups will start to merge and the new families will carry a much higher light. Around 2034, they will be fully enlightened. This will be a very special place to live in peace and joy.

~ Rhode Island ~

The energy here will rise considerably after 2012, bringing an interest in active, passionate hobbies, like salsa dancing for example. This will bring aliveness to this area, and the Earth itself will throb with it. The vibration will spread for a thousand miles in all directions, touching and enlivening all humans and animals. Rhode Island will be a charismatic, lively and exciting area to live in.

~ South Carolina ~

Like North Carolina, this area needs cleansing and is likely to be affected by flooding. The people in South Carolina are strong and resilient. The experience will open their hearts, help them dissolve the karma of the past and become tolerant and loving.

~ South Dakota ~

As with North Dakota this state is deeply affected by the cosmic portal of Hollow Earth, which brings in the light of the twelve rays, the divine feminine and the Christ light. The energy of love and truth from this portal will flow everywhere, dissolving the old and helping people to fulfil their destinies.

People will find themselves drawn to South Dakota, because its underlying energy is very friendly. It will eventually become a golden area, but not a Golden City. In 2012 when the portal opens, Seraphim with their extraordinary high frequency will touch and physically affect people's heart chakras. If people can connect with this area, they will experience illumination and happiness. Their guides will help them to feel deep love and connection with their loved ones. There will be challenges and earth shifts, but this area will eventually radiate light to the world.

~ *Tennessee* ~

Like all the South of the US this state still holds karma from the slave era, though some areas have dissolved much of the energy through subsequent right action. Memphis was a centre for slave trading and the old feelings are still held in the land; however, music has played a part in dissolving some of this in more recent years. An emerald and deep blue energy is dormant within the land waiting to be released in 2012, and Archangels Raphael and Michael will work with this energy to bring healing, abundance and strength to the people here. There may be cleansing by air and water. However, it is anticipated that the citizens will open their minds and hearts to higher spirituality through their connection with the Archangels, so that the transition could be smoother than in other southern states.

~ *Texas* ~

The land here holds the anger and grief of the many Native American tribes forced to move here. The cotton trade was dependent on slavery, and the fear, rage and hopelessness of the slaves is also locked into the land. Drilling for oil has done much damage to Earth itself, who is crying out in pain, and it is essential that this be healed. In addition, the attitude of careless greed is affecting the area, as is spiritual misunderstanding about the use of guns and religious dogma. This is all waiting to be cleansed. This area will be considerably shaken up before it emerges at a higher level of light.

~ *Utah* ~

This is a beautiful place where people are very courageous and generous in many ways. Where the land has been under snow it has been purified. Different animals will migrate here, driven by the Earth changes and climate. As people start to realize the importance of birds and animals and the land itself, attitudes will change and this area will rise in frequency. Yellowstone is a huge portal bringing in love of nature. The super volcano is not expected to erupt during the transition years.

~ Vermont ~

This is what the angels describe as the 'State of the Children' because of the purity and innocence held in the land itself. This energy seeps into the people who live here, keeping everything at a higher level. After 2012, people can mentally align themselves to the energy of Vermont to bring themselves into oneness. An easy transition for this beautiful area.

~ Virginia ~

This state houses many students and other people engaged in learning. They will be inspired by spirit, enabling them to bring forward their talents and strengthen their personalities. They will put their knowledge to practical use in a good way for the benefit of everyone.

The weather may be unsettled but there is angelic influence and protection here. The people have courage and higher qualities, which will enable them to make the most of every situation they find themselves in. Many will find their lives changing suddenly, often for the better.

~ Washington ~

Situated in the northwest corner of America, the mountains in Washington are light and mostly clear of karma, for the many Native American tribes who lived here before the settlers arrived truly honoured the Earth. Seattle and the geographically low areas have been kept pure by water flowing around the islands, though much of this will flood. All places with low business ethics will start to disappear during the next twenty years. Washington is under the direct influence of the cosmic portal opening in Banff, Canada, where Archangel Michael has been holding the energy and keeping it strong. This will help this state to have the confidence and courage to do what is for the highest good.

~ West Virginia ~

Though there are many energies and much unconditional love available to help us, we have to do our part to reach the higher dimensions. West Virginia carries special qualities to enable people to ground the light. When you tune into here, it will also help you to clear your heart, so that you can open it fully. This beautiful area will slip easily into the new age.

~ Wisconsin ~

All karma held here is being dissolved. The angels are working with the people in Wisconsin to remove guilt and self-blame, so that they can make a fresh start. They will only receive this grace, when they are ready to accept it. Then they will evolve into a higher frequency, working with the land and animals, and this will become a loving and light place to live in.

~ Wyoming ~

Lying to the west of the cosmic portal of Hollow Earth, this state will be affected when it opens. In addition, a sacred portal can be found below the mountains in Wyoming. It was set by beings from Orion, the planet of wisdom and enlightenment, who travelled here to prepare this place for the future. This portal will take away heavier energies and transmute them. When they have been transformed into a gentle light, they are showered back over the land. This soft feminine force can then be projected to the waters and all creatures in them. As the ice melts, the blessed water will flow in the oceans and rivers. It will change people's attitude to animals and to the land, and help with the transition.

CHAPTER 20

The Caribbean

~ Barbados and St. Kitts ~

The residents of these islands are fun-loving and forgiving. The karma within the land caused by slavery will be cleansed by light from the people, especially through drumming and music.

The people here crave to be educated and empowered. Some turn to crime because they have a need to be valued. For this to happen, they need the world to send in light, so that they create jobs internally and build peace and prosperity for themselves. This will be considerably influenced by the fact that these islands are on a significant ley line carrying peace and prosperity. In addition, the drinking water of Barbados is filtered through coral, which fills it with fifth-dimensional energy.

~ Cuba ~

When this island received its big challenge, the energy became polarized. The energy in Havana is very dark, while in the countryside it is very light. The dark areas will be cleansed by hurricane.

~ Jamaica ~

Several people have asked me what underlies the violence in this beautiful but troubled island. Jamaica was originally populated by gentle, open-hearted Arawak Indians. They were enslaved by the invading Spaniards and all died of ill-treatment and broken hearts within fifty years. The Spaniards replaced them with slaves from Africa, who were also harshly treated. The feelings of fear, heartbreak and loss, together with the fighting that ensued over the centuries have been locked into the land. Much of this has been transmuted in the seventeenth century by earthquake, flood and fire but by no means all of it.

Jamaica lies exactly between the cosmic portals opening in Honduras and the Bermuda Triangle and is affected by both their energies. This has resulted in a detox taking place, so that all the old anger is rising up to be cleared. This is the underlying cause of all the violence.

In addition, the cosmic heart centre of the planet in Guatemala is beginning to shine and this influences the people of Jamaica. By 2022, this country will radiate the most beautiful pink aura and will be a refuge and haven for many.

~ *Trinidad* ~

Trinidad holds deep karma and some anger from the time of slavery. The people have lost their way at a soul level. They feel disempowered and there is a great deal of crime because of drugs and hopelessness. The land needs cleansing and some of this will be done by the music they love to create. However, this island will be cleansed by water and hurricane, unless enough people send in light.

SECTION 3

Preparation for The Transition

How to Prepare Yourself for The Transition into The Golden Age

~ Purification ~

Whenever you feel grumpy, worried, irritable, easily annoyed or upset by others, disgruntled that you are not receiving what you deserve or that life is unfair, you need purification before you can raise your energy. Here are some suggestions.

EXERCISE 1: *Nature*

- Go out into nature. If possible walk in trees, or by water, or barefoot in the grass. Mentally ask nature to transmute your lower energies.
- Hug a tree. Visualize roots from your feet linking with the roots of the tree and imagine all your discordant energy draining away through them.

EXERCISE 2: *The gold and silver violet flame of transmutation*

This flame is one of the most powerful of all transmuting energies. It opens you up so you must place a protection around yourself before you invoke it. Then it will cleanse your aura and your cells. You can also send it to others to help them.

During sleep, your spirit leaves its physical sheath and journeys into the inner planes. Often you go to your home planet for spiritual comfort and sustenance, but you may go to many realms for guidance, help, to give or receive healing, and wisdom. Before you start your practice decide where you want your spirit to go, for example to a special portal, to the retreat of a Master or Archangel or to another planet for give or receive teaching, healing, wisdom or service. If you have heard of a disaster or tragedy, you may offer to serve during your sleep.

1. Place your protection around you as you do in the morning.
2. Invoke Archangel Sandalphon to place his fifth-dimensional bubble over you and anyone who has asked you. They must be ready to receive this and ask for it. Ask his angels to stand at your gate and place a fifth-dimensional bubble over anyone who enters.
3. Then you may choose to do any or all of the following:
   - Send love and healing to individuals and places.
   - Send angels of peace to parts of the world that need it.
   - Name the place you wish to visit in your sleep and ask to receive the highest.
   - Ask your dragon, who is a fourth-dimensional elemental, to accompany you to burn away any lower energies that might impede your flight.
   - Offer yourself in service during your sleep.
     Ask to receive healing and be prepared to return energized for your day.
   - Ask the unicorns to balance your twelve fifth-dimension chakras.
   - Ask the angels to sing over you while you sleep.
   - When you close your eyes, know that your sleep time is as important spiritually as anything you do during the day. It is an extraordinary opportunity to accelerate your spiritual growth and ascension and a time when you can really help others.

~ Raising Your Spirits ~

It is very easy to get stressed in these days of fast everything, and stress creates low feelings and energies. Also all the things that we have not dealt with, including those from our teens and childhood as well as past lives, is being brought to our attention. This is a huge time for emotional clearance and release. Here are some ways of clearing out the old and raising your spirits when you need to.

~ Nature ~

I was feeling very down one morning. One of my daughters had a go at me about something in her childhood and I let it get to me, so I was doing a number on myself as I churned and felt angry and upset. I decided to walk in my local forest and let the trees help me. It was sunny with a cool nip in the air and I said, "Nature, I surrender these feelings to you."

Almost immediately I became aware of a fairy sitting on my shoulder. I asked her to sing but I could not hear her, which was frustrating and I knew it was because of my low energy. I felt there were many elementals around me including Gobolino, my wonderful goblin friend. All at once they all joined together and sang my name with great love and caring, and this time I could hear it. The angels joined them and then a unicorn added light. I felt as if heaven was pouring waves and waves of love into me as they sang "Diana… Diana… Diana…" over and over again.

When they had finished there was a moment of silence. Then a message was called to me. "Forgive the person you were then and rejoice in who you are now."

Hours later, I could feel the warmth in my heart and the old stuck feelings totally left me. In fact, later that day I tried to recall what had upset me so much and it simply was no longer there.

One of the best ways of letting go of the old and raising your spirits is to go to a pine forest or the ocean and offer them the lower feelings. If you let go, they will then hold you in the fifth dimension.

~ *The Elements* ~

Water, air, fire and earth all offer deep cleansing and connect you with higher energies that can bring you into joyous alignment with your life. All the elements have cosmic qualities, and when you understand this and breathe them into your cells you can profoundly transform your conditions. Currently, we are not skilled at working with water, air, fire and earth so we do not recognize their power. However, when the cleansing comes to the planet we need to understand them so that we can utilize their gifts.

Remember that the faster your frequency, the less affected you are by the elements, so if a storm is forecast, raise your vibration.

One evening there was a storm in the air and Lady Gaia came in to talk about it. She said the destruction by tornadoes that had recently taken place in the US would have been much less if people had connected to the air elementals, the sylphs, and to the Elemental Master in charge of them, called Dom.

The unicorns are in charge of air so we can connect with them, tell them what we want air to do and ask them to supervise this. If enough people had quietly asked the sylphs to cleanse gently and bring in qualities of enlightenment and the ability to see a higher perspective, there would have been no destruction in America and the people would have moved along their ascension pathway.

We need to know what we want. So another example would be if school pupils are dejected by the systems in schools, ask the unicorns and Dom to bring a breeze carrying the air quality of enthusiasm to touch them. At the same time call this breeze in around the Minister of Education to bring inspiration and wisdom to him.

We can use the element of air to spread angel singing round the world.

To help asthma sufferers, we can send a prayer to the unicorns and the Elemental Master, Dom, to purify the air and ask the sylphs to spread this cleansed air before we breathe it.

Angels and other seventh-dimensional beings are the essence of the energy vibration of air. They only want the highest good. If you are scared of a storm, you are not embracing these seventh-dimensional beings. When you walk in a breeze, you can feel the cobwebs being blown away but it is much more than that, for here you have an opportunity to work with the cosmic forces.

When we send out low frequencies it creates a blockage in the flow. It may, for example, block a ley line. As the energy of the planet gets faster, it pushes the blockage out and this may result in an earthquake as it did in Haiti. However, if we send seventh-dimensional light or angels into a blockage, it dissolves gently. In this way we have the power to prevent much damage.

– When we hold things down through worry we hold the potential of air down. When we raise the frequency, we are set free on every level. Gravity is connected to the lower frequencies and as we ascend we move beyond gravity into space. The gifts many had in the Golden Era of Atlantis are fifth- to seventh-dimensional aspects of air, for example telepathy or levitation. As we work with the sylphs, Dom and the Unicorns we bring this back, for we are aligning with the wisdom within the air. We can ask air to heal the minds of people so that they can communicate at a higher frequency and bring telepathy forward.
– If you want to let go of the old and raise your spirits, have a bath, shower, swim or walk by water. Bless it. Then ask it to wash away the old and replace it with higher qualities.
– Earth loves you. When you walk on the planet, you are being held with caring and tenderness. If you walk in bare feet you make a connection that enables the Earth to take in your old feelings and fill you with joy. The Earth helps you to be grounded, nurturing, and capable, and to bring forward ancient wisdom.
– Fire transmutes the old very powerfully. Write down your old feelings and burn them, then breathe in the higher qualities of fire such as enthusiasm, inspiration, deservingness and vitality. When you write a letter to someone and then burn it, it has a huge energetic impact because of the cosmic qualities and wisdom held within fire.

~ Singing and Chanting ~

We take in deeper breaths when we sing or chant, so with this we are taking in more of the energy of God. Singing and chanting with others also helps to bring us into harmony and attunement with the people and situations around us.

~ A Child Laughing ~

The sound that unlocks one of the Keys to the Universe, that to the portal of Hollow Earth, is innocent laughter, like that of an infant laughing. It is a vibration of pure joy and whenever I hear it I find myself smiling and feeling happy.

EXERCISE 1: *How to raise the frequency of religion to spirituality*

Dogma is fear. Spirituality is love. Terrorism and talk of the fear of God committed or spoken in the name of religion arise from the collective fear of those trying to control with fear. That is no longer acceptable and must be healed for the new Golden Age. You can support this in the following ways:

- Place the name of the religion or action onto photographs of Orbs of the Archangels Uriel, Butyalil, Gabriel, Michael, Metatron, of a unicorn and of Mother Mary.
- Invoke these mighty beings and ask them to transmute dogma within religions and raise the energy to one of love and inspiration.

EXERCISE 2: *Visualization to raise Dogma to Spirituality*

Decide if you wish to send this energy to one religion or all the religions of the world.

1. Find a place where you can be quiet and undisturbed.
2. Light a candle if possible.

3. Close your eyes and relax for a few moments.
4. Ask Archangel Michael to place his deep blue cloak of protection around you.
5. Invoke the love, healing, wisdom and protection of the Christ Light to surround you.
6. Invoke the golden Archangel Uriel and sense him by you.
7. Invoke the pure white light of the Universal Angel Butyalil and sense him by you.
8. Invoke the pure white light of Archangel Gabriel and sense him by you.
9. Invoke the deep blue light of Archangel Michael and sense him by you.
10. Invoke the orange light of Archangel Metatron and sense him by you.
11. Invoke a pure white unicorn and sense him by you.
12. Invoke the aquamarine light of the Universal Angel Mother Mary and sense her by you.
13. Visualize a huge book containing all the human-made laws of religion. See these mighty angels pouring their love, light, wisdom and compassion into the book until it disappears and transforms into a huge pink white rose radiating pure love.
14. See the angels flying over all religious establishments and placing the rose of higher spirituality into the auras above the buildings.
15. See the minds and hearts of dogmatic people everywhere opening and becoming golden.
16. Open yourself to receive a blessing.
17. Thank the universal angels and open your eyes.

~ How to Heal the Planet ~

EXERCISE 1: *How to help clear the karma of a country*

It is the mark of a fifth-dimensional person that they want to help others as well as themselves and other countries as well as their own recognizing we are all part of the whole.

- Light a candle and ask the angels to heal and transmute old energies within the country.
- Send the Gold and Silver Violet Flame surrounded by a circle of golden Christ Light with a six-pointed star in the centre of it to the country or place it on a map. This is a very powerful transmuting symbol, which clears any ancient karma from Atlantis.
- Visualize the light flowing along the ley lines under the place.
- Invoke the mighty Universal Angel Butyalil who is in charge of the cosmic currents to sing over the country.

EXERCISE 2: *How to send positive energy to a place or country*

- Visualize bubbles of love touching the people here.
- Ask the angels of peace and love to sing over a country.
- Bless the leaders and the people with joy, peace, integrity, abundance, wisdom and any other qualities they may need.
- Light a candle and send the higher qualities of the fire element to inspire and raise the people.
- Ask a unicorn to take the higher qualities of air, such as enlightenment and ascension to the country.

EXERCISE 3: *Visualization to heal the planet*

1. Find a place where you can be quiet and undisturbed.
2. Light a candle if possible.
3. Close your eyes and relax for a few moments.
4. Ask Archangel Michael to place his deep blue cloak of protection around you.
5. Invoke the love, healing, wisdom and protection of the Christ Light to surround you.
6. Invite a pure white unicorn to approach you. Feel its love and wondrous light, then let it pour love and enlightenment over you from its horn.
7. Sit on its back as it rises above the planet.
8. Be aware that beautiful angels of every colour surround you.

9. Let the unicorn take you to a place that needs peace and healing. Ask it to send balls of pure white light down into the land below you. Imagine the people and the land absorbing it and opening up.
10. Ask the angels to sing of peace and harmony and the air elementals to spread this round the world. Take a few moments to listen to this, and know that even if the sound is beyond your auditory range it is happening.
11. Ask the mighty angels to join together and send light from their different rays into the ley lines of the planet. Watch the web of energy lighting up.
12. Imagine the entire planet radiating a golden light ready to enter the new Golden Age.
13. Relax as the unicorn glides back with you to where you started.
14. Thank him and the angels.
15. Open your eyes and accept the gratitude of the spiritual realms.

Epilogue

Our guides and angels are constantly asking us to celebrate how much we have achieved so far. Our planet and most of us have moved from the third to the fourth dimension, and many are already living in the fifth dimension! It is quite outstanding to make such a shift in such a short space of time. The spiritual world is rejoicing and cheering us on.

You came to experience a unique journey on Earth, so celebrate how far you have come. When you see the numbers 11.11, it is a reminder that you have moved a step higher.

During the transition, you and the entire world will be catching glimpses of the glorious future, a time when we will all live with open hearts, see the best in others and trust the universe to support us.

Because the new emphasis will be on creativity, sharing, caring and co-operating for the highest good, you will feel safe and supported by family, friends and neighbours.

With the opening of the cosmic portals, you may experience true family harmony and love with a sense of personal freedom. You will be able to be yourself and will be encouraged to do what brings your soul satisfaction. For the first time since Atlantis, you will have a chance to experience true deep inner happiness and contentment. If that is already your reality, rejoice that you have come so far.

You will take total responsibility for all you have created and use your mastery to manifest an abundant, joy-filled life for yourself, do what makes you feel fulfilled, develop your talents and live in harmony. With an open heart you will want to enable others to bring forward their hidden gifts too.

As you become increasingly more in touch with nature, you will sense the wisdom and love reaching out to you from trees and flowers, and experience the extraordinary cosmic energy of the seas and rivers. As you walk, you will be aware of the elementals and how they support nature and the life force and well-being of Earth. You will feel their lightness and their love for you as well as the love of the planet.

Spiritual technology will start to be used, and this will expand our consciousness as well as ease our lives. One example of this are the digital cameras built to capture the light of the angelic realms as Orbs. As more light rises during and after 2012, spiritual technology will start to influence travel, power, communication and weather control in ways that are currently beyond our comprehension. Computers will use faster frequencies and carry light information, enabling instant global communication and facilitating understanding between cultures and countries. Technology will be balanced by the closer connection with nature.

Once again people are recognizing the possibilities held within crystals. As we respect them and start to work with them from the heart, we will be able to unleash their power with wisdom.

The Orbs have enabled more people to believe in angels and attune to the angelic realms, and this understanding and belief will rapidly increase. Then, as a world, we will invoke and receive more assistance from the angelic and unicorn realms. This will hugely light up the possibilities for our lives. How wonderful when everyone walks with angels and Masters! As this happens, more are making their connections with the seventh-dimensional centre of our planet known as Hollow Earth, and this is accelerating us into higher ascension.

Already we are seeing new high-frequency businesses being developed, which are succeeding because their motivation is to do what is for the highest good, helping animals, people and nature. These will increase and grow in service to everyone.

Women everywhere are beginning to stand in their power. They are recognizing their own light. At the same time some religions will soon open up to spirituality, which will soften dogma. This will allow people to come together and to honour and respect each others' cultures.

As the consciousness of the Western world rises, more people are embracing higher healing methods. There is less reliance on allopathic drugs as a cure-all, and those who have cleared much of the karmic component of their illness are seeking more natural methods of balancing themselves. The interest in maintaining health through crystals, herbs, flower essences, Reiki and spiritual healing, sound and many other ways will continue to increase.

The power of sound to bring into harmony and peace and even facilitate deep healing is being recognized. Sound and sacred geometry will increasingly be used to maintain a fifth-dimensional frequency within communities.

Waves of high-frequency, spiritual children are being born. They are coming in from all the universes and are prepared to serve during the transition. They carry extraordinary light, knowledge, information and wisdom. Many are wired with important spiritual technology to help us all into the new Golden Age. The more we can raise our frequency to the fifth dimension and hold it there, the more of these souls can come in and truly express their encoded gifts. Already some are being born who carry the new blueprint for humans and for the planet. If the new children have fifth-dimensional parents, their possibilities are limitless.

Every day, the number of people rising to and maintaining a fifth-dimensional frequency is increasing. When enough people do so, we will have world peace and co-operation. We will live in a world without boundaries, where all are abundant. Our future is golden.

You are asked to remind yourself what an amazing job you have done so far and congratulate yourself for handling change so well. The final message from the angels is 'celebrate yourself'. Celebrate who you are. Celebrate your life and your mission. You have done exceptionally well, and the angels and unicorns are singing over you to encourage and applaud you. They send their gratitude.

Appendix

~ *The 12 Spiritual Chakras of the Planet* ~

CHAKRA	LOCATION
1. Earth Star chakra	London, United Kingdom
2. Base chakra	Gobi Desert, China
3. Sacral chakra	Honolulu, Hawaii
4. Navel chakra	Fiji
5. Solar Plexus chakra	The whole of South Africa
6. Heart chakra	Glastonbury, United Kingdom
7. Throat chakra	Luxor, Egypt
8. Third Eye chakra	Afghanistan
9. Crown chakra	Machu Picchu, Peru
10. Causal chakra	Tibet
11. Soul Star chakra	Agra, India
12. Stellar Gateway chakra	Arctic

~ *The 12 Spiritual Chakras of the Planet* ~

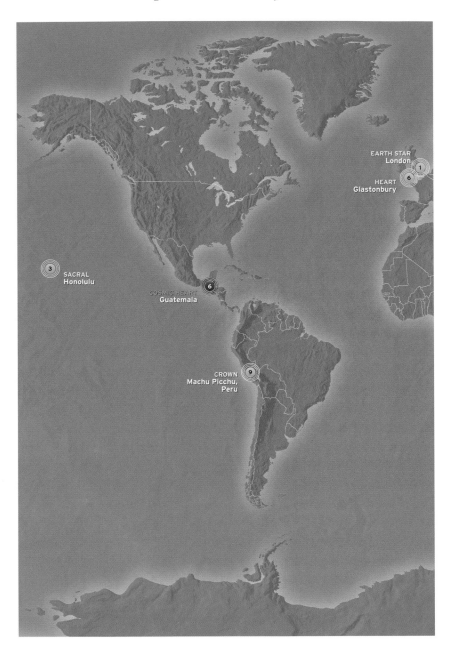

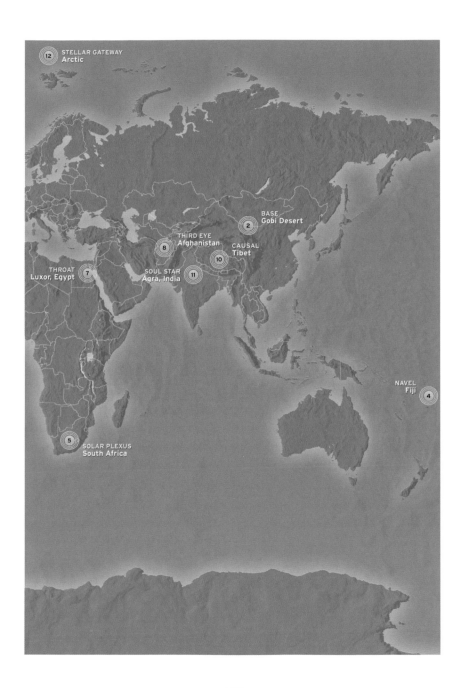

~ *The 33 Cosmic Portals* ~

PORTAL	TIME OF OPENING
ANCIENT CULTURES	
1. Atlantis – Atlantic Ocean	Already opening
2. Lemuria – Hawaii	Already opening
3. Hollow Earth – Oklahoma, Kansas, Nebraska, South Dakota, southern North Dakota	Already opening
4. Mu – Pacific Ocean	In 2012
AUSTRALASIA	
5. Aborigine Wisdom – Uluru, Australia	In 2012
6. Maori Wisdom – Fiji	In 2012
AMERICAS	
7. Native American Wisdom – Sedona, USA	In 2012
8. Great Crystal of Atlantis – Bermuda Triangle	Alternates between open and closed
9. Banff, Canada	In 2012
10. Inuit Wisdom – Alaska, Arctic	In 2012
11. South Pole	In 2012
South America	
12. Maya Wisdom – Honduras	Already opening
13. Inca Wisdom – Peru	In 2012
AFRICA	
14. Dogon Wisdom – Mali	In 2012
15. Sphinx – Egypt	In 2012

PORTAL	TIME OF OPENING
THE MIDDLE EAST	
16. Mesopotamia	After 2012
THE FAR EAST	
17. The Source of the Ganges, India	Before 2012
18. Varanasi, India	Already opening
19. Manila, Philippines	In 2012
20. Mongolia	In 2012
21. Angkor Wat, Cambodia	Before 2012
22. Quan Yin - Along the Silk Road	In 2012
23. Wuham, Eastern China	From 2012 to 2014
24. Ansi, Northern China	In 2012
EUROPE	
25. York, Yorkshire Dales, UK	In 2012
26. Andorra	In 2012
27. Off the coast of Marseilles, underwater	Soon after 2012
RUSSIA	
28. Omsk, Urals	In 2012
29. Siberia	In 2012
30. Agata, Northern Russia	In 2014
31. Opala, Kamchatka Island	In 2014
32. Gora Chen, Kerkeyansk Range	Already opening
33. North Pole, Arctic	Already opening

~ *The 33 Cosmic Portals* ~

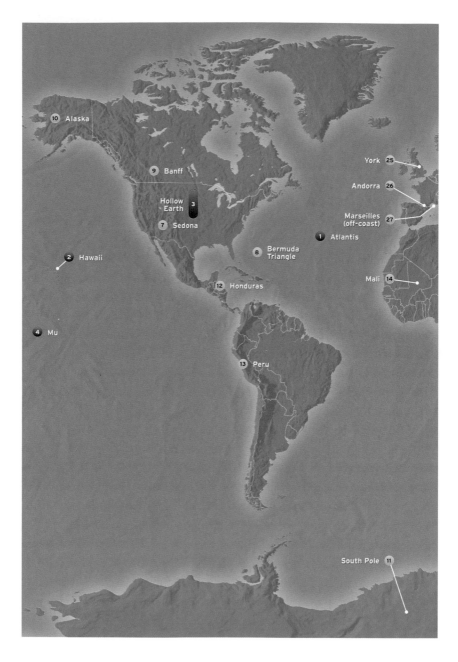

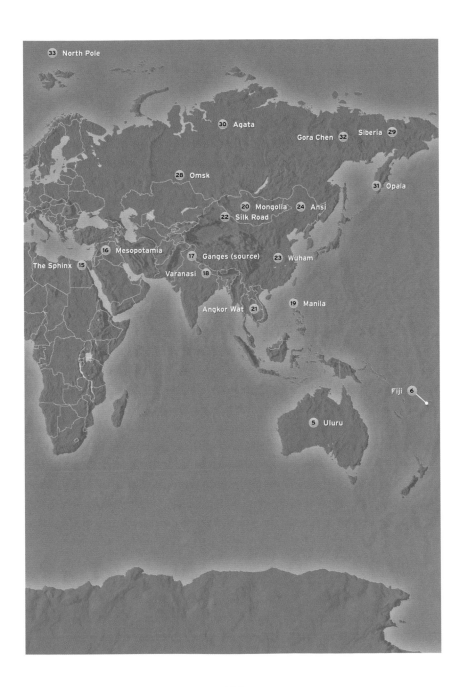

Angels of Light Cards

by

DIANA COOPER

Angels are waiting and happy to help you at all times. Under Spiritual Law they cannot step in until you ask. Whenever you have a problem, there is an angel standing by you, awaiting your permission to assist.

Angels cannot and will not help you if you ask for something from neediness and greed. Nor will they help you receive something which is not spiritually right. Recognize your authority and make your requests from wisdom and strength. You may also ask the angels to help someone else for his or her highest good, not necessarily for what you think that highest good might be. Your thoughts to that person create a rainbow bridge along which the angels can travel to help him or her.

You can also ask the angels to help the planet.

Each of the 52 Angel Cards included in this deck represent a different Angel quality, and can be used for guidance, inspiration and affirmation. The cards will help you tune in to the higher vibrations of the Angels, and allow you to feel the helping hands of these beings at all times. Following the inspiration of the Angels will raise your consciousness, which will automatically help you attract to yourself people and situations of a higher vibratory level and release old negative thought patterns. Carry these cards with you wherever you go and use them to remind yourself of the presence, guidance and help of the Angels in your life, always and everywhere. You are never alone or lost when the Angels are with you.

Set of 52 cards + 2 instructions cards
in desktop presentation stand with slipcase – ISBN 978-1-84409-141-6
***Pocket edition:** set of 52 cards + 2 instructions cards*
in tuckbox – ISBN 978-1-84409-171-3

A New Light on Angels

by

DIANA COOPER

Completely revised, updated and expanded edition of the bestselling *A Little Light on Angels* with new original colour illustrations by Damian Keenan.

"I believe in angels" is the title of a well-known song – but do we really? With this book, we meet everyday folks who have experienced angels in their lives. Yes, angels do exist: they are highly evolved beings that have a lighter and faster vibration than humans, and are normally invisible to us. However, many of them have chosen to serve mankind and are available to help, support, heal and guide us – all we have to do is ask! There are small angels who care for the little daily tasks and enormous beings that overlight great universal projects. There are angels who can assist in healing and other who attend celebrations and rituals.

With close to 50% new materials including new stories, new visualizations and new information on Archangels, this edition of *A New Light on Angels* gives us guidance on how we can call on them for help and companionship in our lives. We are surrounded by angels, all we have to do is raise our consciousness to become aware of them and communicate with them, to welcome them into our lives and allow the joy, light and peace of their presence into our hearts.

"This whole matter of dealing with angels is far more business-like than the unitiated might think, and it is not just about peace, healing and a healthy aura. Angels can also be called upon to solve practical problems, and there is even an angel of parking spaces."

— RONALD WHITE, THE SUNDAY TIMES

144 pages paperback, full colour, illustrated
ISBN 978-1-84409-166-9